Wonton
Cookbook

An Alternative Dumpling Cookbook with Delicious Dumpling Recipes

By
BookSumo Press

Published by
http://www.booksumo.com

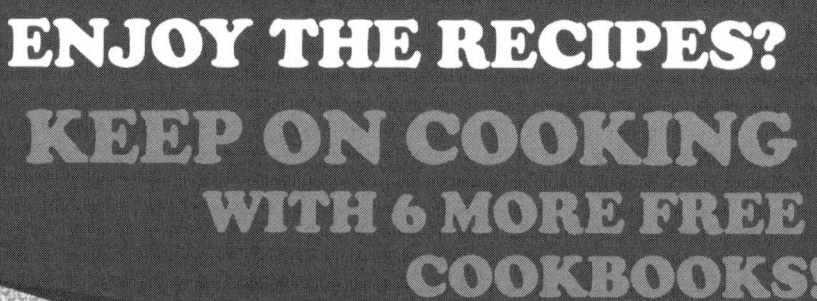

LEGAL NOTES

Table of Contents

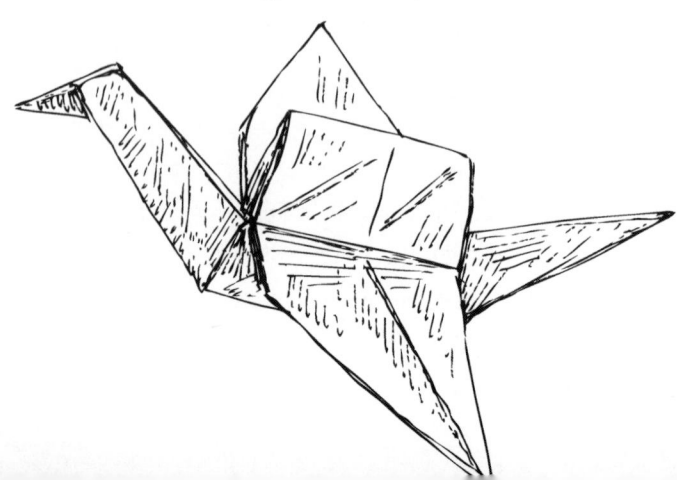

Catalina's
Spicy Wontons

🥣 Prep Time: 20 mins
🕐 Total Time: 20 mins

Servings per Recipe: 15
Calories	685.4
Fat	66.0g
Cholesterol	26.0mg
Sodium	263.0mg
Carbohydrates	18.9g
Protein	5.8g

Ingredients

1 (8 oz.) packages cream cheese, softened
1 C. Monterey Jack cheese, shredded
1 (4 oz.) cans jalapeño peppers, diced
1 tsp minced garlic
3 green onions, diced
black pepper

1 (16 oz.) packages wonton wrappers
1 quart vegetable oil

Directions

1. In a bowl, add the Monterey Jack cheese, cream cheese, green onions, garlic, jalapeño peppers and black pepper and mix until well combined.
2. Place 1 tsp of the jalapeño mixture in the center of each wonton wrapper.
3. With wet fingers, moisten the edges of each wrapper and then, fold over the filling in a triangle shape.
4. Now, with your fingers, press the edges to seal completely.
5. In a skillet, add the oil over medium-high heat and cook until heated through.
6. Add the wontons in batches and cook until golden brown completely, flipping occasionally.
7. With a slotted spoon, transfer the wrappers onto a paper towel-lined plate to drain.
8. Enjoy.

MANITOBA
Maple Wontons

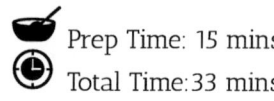
Prep Time: 15 mins
Total Time: 33 mins

Servings per Recipe: 1

Calories	45.1
Fat	0.1g
Cholesterol	0.7mg
Sodium	83.7mg
Carbohydrates	10.1g
Protein	0.9g

Ingredients
1 C. canned pumpkin
2 tbsp maple syrup
3 tbsp brown sugar
1 tsp pumpkin pie spice
16 packaged wonton wrappers
granulated sugar
ground cinnamon
cooking spray

Directions
1. Set your oven to 400 degrees F before doing anything else.
2. In a bowl, add the pumpkin, pumpkin pie spice, brown sugar and maple syrup and mix until well combined.
3. Place about 1 tbsp of the pumpkin mixture in the center of each wonton wrapper.
4. With wet fingers, moisten the edges of each wrapper and then, fold over the filling in a triangle shape.
5. Now, with your fingers, press the edges to seal completely.
6. In the bottom of an ungreased baking sheet, arrange the wonton wrappers and spray with the cooking spray.
7. Dust the wontons with the cinnamon and granulated sugar and cook in the oven for about 16 minutes.
8. Carefully, flip the side and cook in the oven for about 2 minutes.
9. Remove from the oven and keep aside to cool.
10. Enjoy.

Silver Dragon
Wonton Soup

Prep Time: 20 mins
Total Time: 28 mins

Servings per Recipe: 6
Calories   123.1
Fat   3.5g
Cholesterol   13.7mg
Sodium   973.7mg
Carbohydrates   11.2g
Protein   10.4g

Ingredients

2 green onions
1/4 lb. lean ground beef
1/4 C. chopped celery
1 tbsp chopped parsley
1/4 tsp salt
1 dash pepper
12-18 wonton skins

6 C. chicken broth
1/2 C. spinach, shredded
1/4 C. shredded carrot

Directions

1. Remove the top from 1 green onion and cut into thin slices diagonally.
2. Reserve the slices for garnishing.
3. Then, cut the remaining green onions into small pieces.
4. In a bowl, add the ground beef, celery, chopped onion, parsley, salt and pepper and gently, stir to combine.
5. Place about 1 1/2 tbsp of the beef mixture in the center of each wonton square.
6. With wet fingers, moisten the edges of each wrapper and then, fold over the filling in a triangle shape.
7. Now, with your fingers, press the edges to seal completely.
8. In a pan, add the broth and cook until boiling.
9. Now, set the heat to medium.
10. Add the wontons in 2 batches and cook for about 4 minutes.
11. With a slotted spoon, transfer the wontons onto a plate and with a piece of foil, cover them to keep warm.
12. In hot broth, add the spinach, carrot and reserved green onion slices and stir to combine.
13. Divide the wontons into serving bowls and top with the hot broth mixture.
14. Enjoy hot.

ARTISANAL
Wonton Tins

Prep Time: 30 mins
Total Time: 60 mins

Servings per Recipe: 48
Calories	67.3
Fat	3.4g
Cholesterol	7.4mg
Sodium	141.5mg
Carbohydrates	6.5g
Protein	2.8g

Ingredients

1 C. freshly grated Parmesan cheese
1 C. mayonnaise
1/2 tsp onion powder
1/2 tsp garlic powder
2 C. shredded mozzarella cheese
1 (14 oz.) cans water-packed artichoke
hearts, drained and chopped
1 (12 oz.) packages wonton wrappers

Directions

1. Set your oven to 350 degrees F before doing anything else.
2. In a bowl, add the mayonnaise, Parmesan cheese, garlic powder and onion powder and mix until blended nicely.
3. Add the artichoke pieces and mozzarella cheese and mix well.
4. With the cooking spray, spray one side of all wonton wrappers.
5. Place 1 wrapper into 1 of each mini muffin cup and press to fit in a cup shape.
6. Cook in the oven for about 5 minutes.
7. Remove from the oven and place 1 tbsp of the artichoke mixture in each cup.
8. Cook in the oven for about 5-6 minutes.
9. Enjoy warm.

How to Make
Wonton Wraps

🥣 Prep Time: 1 hr 30 mins
🕐 Total Time: 1 hr 30 mins

Servings per Recipe: 1
Calories	981.5
Fat	7.2g
Cholesterol	186.0mg
Sodium	1242.3mg
Carbohydrates	191.1g
Protein	32.1g

Ingredients

2 C. all-purpose flour
1/2 tsp salt
1 egg
1/4 C. water
1/4 C. water
extra flour

Directions

1. In a bowl, add the flour and salt and mix well.
2. In another bowl, add the egg and 1/4 C. of water and gently, beat until well combined.
3. With your hands, create a well in the center of the flour mixture.
4. Add the egg mixture in the well and mix alongside the remaining water.
5. With your hands, knead the dough until a smooth dough forms.
6. Transfer the dough into a bowl.
7. With a damp cloth, cover the bowl and aside for about 1 hour.
8. Divide the dough into 4 equal sized portions.
9. Place one dough portion onto a generously floured surface and with a rolling pin, roll into a very thin circle.
10. Now, cut the dough into equal sized circles.
11. Repeat with the remaining dough portions.

4-INGREDIENT
Wontons

Prep Time: 5 mins
Total Time: 12 mins

Servings per Recipe: 16
Calories	96.7
Fat	3.1g
Cholesterol	9.0mg
Sodium	91.9mg
Carbohydrates	15.6g
Protein	1.6g

Ingredients
1/2 C. granulated sugar
1 1/2 tsp ground cinnamon
32 wonton wrappers
4 tbsp unsalted butter, melted

Directions
1. Set your oven to 400 degrees F before doing anything else.
2. In a bowl, add the sugar and cinnamon and mix well.
3. Carefully, separate the wonton wrappers.
4. In the bottom of a baking sheets, arrange the wonton wrappers about 1/2-inch apart.
5. Coat each wrapper with the butter evenly and dust with the cinnamon sugar.
6. Cook in the oven for about 5-7 minutes.
7. Remove from the oven and place onto the wire rack to cool.
8. You can preserve these wrappers in an airtight container.

Wontons with Seoul

🥣 Prep Time: 30 mins
🕐 Total Time: 50 mins

Servings per Recipe: 1
Calories   31.5
Fat   1.2g
Cholesterol   5.7mg
Sodium   55.9mg
Carbohydrates   3.7g
Protein   1.2g

Ingredients

2 C. shredded cabbage
1 C. canned bean sprouts
1/2 C. shredded carrot
1 1/2 tsp vegetable oil, plus
2 tbsp vegetable oil, divided
1/3 lb. ground beef
1/3 C. green onion, sliced
1 1/2 tsp sesame seeds, toasted

1/2 tsp ground ginger
3 cloves garlic, minced
1 1/2 tsp sesame oil
1/2 tsp salt
1/2 tsp pepper
1 (12 oz.) packages wonton wrappers
1 egg, beaten
3 tbsp water

Directions

1. Heat a skillet and cook the ground beef until done completely.
2. Drain the grease from the skillet.
3. Meanwhile, in another skillet, add 1 1/2 tsp of the oil and cook until heated through.
4. Add the carrot, cabbage and bean sprouts and sauté until tender.
5. Add the cooked beef, green onions, garlic, sesame oil, sesame seeds, ground ginger, salt and pepper and stir to combine.
6. Remove from the heat.
7. In a bowl, add the egg and water and beat well.
8. Place about 1 tbsp of the beef mixture in the center of each wonton wrapper.
9. With wet fingers, moisten the edges of each wrapper and then, fold over the filling in a triangle shape.
10. Now, with your fingers, press the edges to seal completely.
11. In a wok, add the remaining oil and cook until heated through.
12. Add the wontons in batches and cook for about 2-4 minutes, flipping once half way through.
13. Enjoy warm.

GILROY GARLIC
Festival Wontons

Prep Time: 45 mins
Total Time: 55 mins

Servings per Recipe: 10
Calories	179.9
Fat	8.3g
Cholesterol	28.0mg
Sodium	273.5mg
Carbohydrates	20.9g
Protein	5.1g

Ingredients

1 (8 oz.) packages cold cream cheese
3 garlic cloves (minced)
1 (12 oz.) packages wonton wrappers
1 egg white

Directions

1. In a bowl, add the cream cheese and garlic and mix until well combined.
2. Refrigerate to chill for about 15 minutes
3. Place about 1 tsp of the cream cheese mixture in the center of each wonton wrapper.
4. With wet fingers, moisten the edges of each wrapper and then, fold over the filling in a triangle shape.
5. Now, with your fingers, press the edges to seal completely.
6. Wet each square edge with the egg wash.
7. Fold into triangles.
8. In a deep skillet, add the oil and cook until its temperature reaches to 450 degrees F.
9. Add the wontons in batches and cook until golden brown from both sides.
10. With a slotted spoon, transfer the wontons onto a paper towel-lined plate to drain.
11. Enjoy alongside your favorite dipping sauces.

Southwest
Breakfast Wontons

🥣 Prep Time: 20 mins
🕐 Total Time: 30 mins

Servings per Recipe: 1
Calories	201.3
Fat	13.8g
Cholesterol	24.5mg
Sodium	430.4mg
Carbohydrates	11.9g
Protein	6.5g

Ingredients

1 (16 oz.) packages wonton wrappers
1 lb. beef sausage, browned, drained and cooled
1 C. shredded Monterey Jack cheese
1 C. shredded cheddar cheese
1 C. ranch dressing

Directions

1. Set your oven to 350 degrees F before doing anything else and grease cups of a mini muffin pan.
2. Place 1 wrapper into 1 of each prepared muffin cup and press to fit in a cup shape.
3. Cook in the oven for about 5 minutes.
4. Remove from the oven and keep aide to cool.
5. In a bowl, add the sausage, Ranch dressing and cheeses and mix until well combined.
6. Place the sausage mixture into each cup and cook in the oven for about 10 - 15 minutes.
7. Enjoy warm.

HOT GINGER
Wontons

Prep Time: 10 mins
Total Time: 30 mins

Servings per Recipe: 2
Calories	378.4
Fat	20.9g
Cholesterol	288.0mg
Sodium	1337.8mg
Carbohydrates	4.5g
Protein	43.4g

Ingredients
1 lb. ground chicken
1 large egg
1 tsp ground ginger
3 garlic cloves, minced
1/4 C. green onion, chopped
1/4 tsp allspice
1/8 tsp cinnamon
1/4 tsp cayenne pepper
1 tsp salt

1 tsp pepper
oil

Directions
1. In a bowl, add the egg, chicken, green onion and spices and mix well.
2. In a deep skillet, add the oil and cook until its temperature reaches to 375 degrees F.
3. With 1 tsp, place the mixture and cook until golden brown.
4. With a slotted spoon, transfer the wontons onto a paper towel-lined plate to drain.
5. Enjoy alongside your favorite sauce.

Cream Cheese Dumplings

🥣 Prep Time: 5 mins
🕐 Total Time: 20 mins

Servings per Recipe: 1
Calories   188.1
Fat   6.8g
Cholesterol   36.4mg
Sodium   245.2mg
Carbohydrates   26.9g
Protein   4.6g

Ingredients

1 egg
1 (8 oz.) Philadelphia Cream Cheese
1/2 C. sugar
1 package of wonton wrappers
1 C. water
oil

Directions

1. In a bowl, add the egg and beat well.
2. Add 1/2 C. of the sugar and cream cheese and beat until well combined.
3. Place the mixture into the center of each wonton wrapper.
4. With wet fingers, moisten the edges of each wrapper and then, fold over the filling in a triangle shape.
5. Now, with your fingers, press the edges to seal completely.
6. In a deep skillet, add the oil and cook until heated through.
7. Add the wontons in batches and cook until golden brown from both sides.
8. With a slotted spoon, transfer the wontons onto a paper towel-lined plate to drain.
9. Enjoy warm.

EASY BUFFALO
Wontons

Prep Time: 30 mins
Total Time: 50 mins

Servings per Recipe: 1
Calories   52.6
Fat   2.0g
Cholesterol   11.1mg
Sodium   123.2mg
Carbohydrates   4.7g
Protein   3.4g

Ingredients
2 chicken breasts, cooked and chopped
1/4 C. buffalo-style hot sauce
1/2 tsp chopped garlic
1/4 C. cream cheese
24 wonton wrappers
oil

Directions
1. In a bowl, add the chicken, cream cheese, hot sauce and garlic and ix until smooth.
2. Place about 1 tsp of the chicken mixture in the center of each wonton wrapper.
3. With wet fingers, moisten the edges of each wrapper and then, fold over the filling in a triangle shape.
4. Now, with your fingers, press the edges to seal completely.
5. In a deep skillet, add the oil and cook until its temperature reaches to 325 degrees F.
6. Add the wontons in batches and cook until golden brown from both sides.
7. With a slotted spoon, transfer the wontons onto a paper towel-lined plate to drain.
8. Enjoy hot.

Mozzarella Wonton Bites

🍳 Prep Time: 20 mins
🕐 Total Time: 38 mins

Servings per Recipe: 1
Calories	71.1
Fat	3.4g
Cholesterol	25.8mg
Sodium	164.8mg
Carbohydrates	6.1g
Protein	3.9g

Ingredients

24 square wonton wrappers
1 tbsp butter, melted
10 oz. shelled deveined and cooked medium shrimp
2 green onions, chopped
1/3 C. grated carrot
4 oz. cream cheese, softened
1-2 cloves minced garlic
1/2-1 tsp Worcestershire sauce
1 C. grated mozzarella cheese

Directions

1. Set your oven to 350 degrees F before doing anything else and lightly grease cups of mini muffin pans.
2. Coat one side of each wonton wrapper with the butter evenly.
3. Place 1 wrapper into 1 of each prepared mini muffin cup, buttered-side up and press to fit in a cup shape.
4. Cook in the oven for about 8 minutes.
5. Remove from the oven and keep aside.
6. Place 24 shrimp into a bowl and reserve them.
7. Chop the remaining shrimp finely and place into a second bowl.
8. In a third bowl, add the garlic, cream cheese and Worcestershire sauce and mix till well combined.
9. Add the chopped shrimp, mozzarella cheese, carrot and green onions and mix until well combined.
10. Place the shrimp mixture into each wonton cup evenly and top each with the reserved shrimp.
11. Enjoy.

BAJA
Wontons

🥣 Prep Time: 15 mins
🕐 Total Time: 16 mins

Servings per Recipe: 4
Calories	796.5
Fat	66.5g
Cholesterol	109.0mg
Sodium	833.7mg
Carbohydrates	24.3g
Protein	31.8g

Ingredients
Wontons
1/2 C. canned green chili
1/4 C. canned jalapeño
1 lb. Monterey Jack cheese, shredded
wonton wrapper
Dip
3 avocados
2 tbsp lemon juice
1 tsp seasoning salt, mix

1 tsp ground coriander
1/2 C. mayonnaise
3 green onions, minced

Directions
1. In a food processor, add the Monterey Jack cheese, jalapeño and green chili and pulse until smooth.
2. Place about 2 tbsp of the cheese mixture in the center of each wonton wrapper.
3. With wet fingers, moisten the edges of each wrapper and then, fold over the filling in a triangle shape.
4. Now, with your fingers, press the edges to seal completely.
5. Place about 2 tbsp of the cheese mixture on one corner of the wonton wrapper and fold the corner over the filling.
6. In a deep skillet, add the oil and cook until its temperature reaches to 350 degrees F.
7. Add the wontons in batches and cook for about 2-4 minutes, flipping once half way through.
8. With a slotted spoon, transfer the wontons onto a paper towel-lined plate to drain.
9. Meanwhile, for sauce: in a bowl, add all the ingredients. and mix until well combined.
10. Enjoy the wontons alongside the dipping sauce.

 Wontons
Seattle

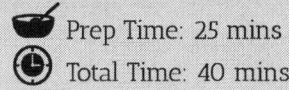

 Prep Time: 25 mins
 Total Time: 40 mins

Servings per Recipe: 1
Calories   50.1
Fat   2.0g
Cholesterol   5.9mg
Sodium   70.5mg
Carbohydrates   6.5g
Protein   1.5g

Ingredients

1/2 tbsp olive oil
1/4 C. onion, chopped
1/4 C. shallot, minced
1 garlic clove, minced
4 oz. cream cheese, softened
1/4 C. mayonnaise
7 oz. quartered artichoke hearts in brine
1/8 tsp ground cayenne pepper

5 oz. frozen chopped spinach, thawed and squeezed dry
1/4 C. grated Asiago cheese
salt
24 wonton wrappers
water
cooking spray

Directions

1. Set your oven to 375 degrees F before doing anything else and arrange a rack in the upper third part of the oven. Lightly, grease a baking sheet.
2. In a skillet, add the oil over medium heat and cook until heated through.
3. Add the shallots and onion and stir fry for about 3 minutes.
4. Stir in the garlic and stir fry for about 20 seconds.
5. Remove from the heat and transfer the onion mixture into a bowl.
6. In a blender, add the artichoke hearts, cream cheese, mayonnaise and cayenne pepper and pulse until smooth.
7. In the bowl of the onion mixture, add the artichoke mixture, spinach, Asiago cheese and salt and mix until well combined.
8. Place about 1/2 tsp of the chocolate chips in the center of each wonton wrapper, followed by 1 strawberry piece.
9. With wet fingers, moisten the edges of each wrapper and then, fold over the filling in a triangle shape.
10. Now, with your fingers, press the edges to seal completely.
11. In the bottom of the prepared baking sheet, arrange the wonton wrappers and spray each with the cooking spray.
12. Cook in the oven for about 10 minutes.
13. Carefully, flip the side and cook for about 4 minutes.
14. Enjoy warm.

WONTONS
West Indian

Prep Time: 15 mins
Total Time: 30 mins

Servings per Recipe: 1

Calories	32.8
Fat	0.1g
Cholesterol	0.6mg
Sodium	40.7mg
Carbohydrates	7.2g
Protein	0.8g

Ingredients
2 large ripe bananas, peeled and cut into slices
24 wonton wrappers
1 tbsp granulated sugar
1/4 tsp ground cinnamon
oil
powdered sugar

Directions
1. In a bowl, add the cinnamon and sugar and mix well.
2. Arrange the wonton wrappers onto a smooth surface.
3. Coat each banana slice with the cinnamon sugar.
4. Place 1 banana slice in the center of each wrapper.
5. With wet fingers, moisten the edges of each wrapper and then, fold over the filling in a triangle shape.
6. Now, with your fingers, press the edges to seal completely.
7. In a deep skillet, add the oil and cook until its temperature reaches to 350 degrees F.
8. Add the wontons in batches and cook until golden brown from both sides.
9. With a slotted spoon, transfer the wontons onto a paper towel-lined plate to drain.
10. Dust with the sugar and enjoy.

Pennsylvania
Park Wontons

🥣 Prep Time: 15 mins
🕐 Total Time: 35 mins

Servings per Recipe: 24
Calories	46.8
Fat	1.4g
Cholesterol	1.7mg
Sodium	49.2mg
Carbohydrates	7.2g
Protein	1.1g

Ingredients

Hershey chocolate kisses
wonton wrappers

confectioners' sugar

Directions

Arrange a chocolate kiss in the middle of each wonton wrapper.

With wet fingers, moisten the edges of each wrapper and then, fold over the filling in a triangle shape.

Now, with your fingers, press the edges to seal completely.

In an electric skillet, add about 1-inch of the oil and cook until its temperature reaches to 375 degrees F.

Add the wontons in batches and cook until golden brown completely.

With a slotted spoon, transfer the wontons onto a paper towel-lined plate to drain.

Sprinkle with the confectioners' sugar and enjoy.

WEEKNIGHT
Ground Beef Wontons

🥣 Prep Time: 30 mins
🕐 Total Time: 40 mins

Servings per Recipe: 6
Calories	928.0
Fat	82.9 g
Cholesterol	75.2m
Sodium	468.2
Carbohydrates	31.0g
Protein	16.0g

Ingredients
1/2 lb. lean ground beef
1/4 C. yellow onion, grated
2 oz. cream cheese
1/4 C. cheddar cheese, shredded
1 large egg
2 tbsp dry breadcrumbs
2 tbsp taco seasoning
2 tbsp cilantro, minced
36 wonton wrappers

1 large egg white, beaten
2 C. canola oil

Directions
1. In a bowl, add the beef, 1 egg, breadcrumbs, cheddar cheese, cream cheese, onion, cilantr and taco seasoning and mix until well combined.
2. Place about 1 tsp of the beef mixture in the center of each wonton wrapper.
3. Coat the edges of wrappers with the beaten egg and fold them over the filling in a triang shape.
4. Now, with your fingers, press the edges to seal completely.
5. In a deep skillet, add the oil and cook until its temperature reaches to 375 degrees F.
6. Add the wontons in batches and cook for about 2 minutes, from both sides.
7. With a slotted spoon, transfer the wontons onto a paper towel-lined plate to drain.
8. Enjoy with a garnishing of the cilantro alongside the salsa.

Hibachi House
Salad with Wonton Crisps

🥣 Prep Time: 20 mins
🕐 Total Time: 25 mins

Servings per Recipe: 8
Calories	391.6
Fat	41.0g
Cholesterol	0.4mg
Sodium	69.1mg
Carbohydrates	6.3g
Protein	1.1g

Ingredients

5 1/2 C. romaine lettuce, torn
2 plum tomatoes, chopped
1/2 C. fresh pineapple, diced
3 tbsp onions, chopped
1 C. vegetable oil
5 wonton wrappers, cut into strips
Dressing
3 tbsp cider vinegar

1/2 tsp ground mustard
1/2 tsp lemon juice
1/8 tsp salt
1 dash pepper
1/2 C. olive oil

Directions

1. In a bowl, add the pineapple, tomatoes, romaine and onion and mix.
2. In a skillet, add the vegetable oil and cook until its temperature reaches to 375 degrees F.
3. Add the wonton strips in batches and cook for about 15-20 seconds.
4. With a slotted spoon, transfer the wontons onto a paper towel-lined plate to drain.
5. Place the strips over the bowl of the salad.
6. In a food processor, add the mustard, vinegar, lemon juice, salt and pepper and pulse until well combined.
7. While motor is running, slowly add the olive oil and pulse until well combined.
8. Drizzle the dressing over the salad and enjoy.

HAPPY WONTONS
with Orange Sauce

Prep Time: 25 mins
Total Time: 45 mins

Servings per Recipe: 1

Calories	52.6
Fat	1.3g
Cholesterol	12.3mg
Sodium	454.3mg
Carbohydrates	7.4g
Protein	2.7g

Ingredients

1 C. low sodium soy sauce
1/3 C. chopped cilantro
24 sprigs cilantro, leaves and tender stems
1 tbsp lemon zest
2 tbsp minced ginger
2 tsp minced ginger
2 tbsp toasted sesame oil
24 large shell-on shrimp
vegetable oil

24 square wonton wrappers
1/4 C. orange juice
3 tbsp lemon juice
2 tbsp orange marmalade
3 tbsp chopped green onions

Directions

1. In a bowl, add 1 tbsp of the sesame oil, 1/2 C. of the soy sauce, cilantro, 2 tbsp of the ginger and lemon zest and beat until well combined.

2. Add the shrimp and coat with the mixture generously.

3. Cover the bowl and keep aside for about 18-20 minutes.

4. In a colander, place the shrimp and keep aside until drained completely.

5. With the paper towels, pat dry the shrimp completely.

6. Place the cilantro and leaves stems in the center of each wonton wrapper evenly, followed by 1 shrimp lengthwise.

7. With wet fingers, moisten the edges of each wrapper and then, fold over the filling in a triangle shape.

8. Now, with your fingers, press the edges to seal completely.

9. In a deep skillet, add the oil and cook until its temperature reaches to 375 degrees F.

10. Add the wontons in batches and cook until golden brown from both sides.

11. With a slotted spoon, transfer the wontons onto a paper towel-lined plate to drain.

12. For the dipping sauce: in a bowl, add the remaining ingredients and mix until well combined.

13. Enjoy the wonton wrappers alongside the sauce.

Wontons
Chips with Style

Prep Time: 5 mins
Total Time: 20 mins

Servings per Recipe: 6
Calories   688.4
Fat   7.7g
Cholesterol   19.2mg
Sodium   1450.6mg
Carbohydrates   130.6g
Protein   21.3g

Ingredients

Teriyaki Style
20 - 22 egg roll wraps
2 tbsp teriyaki sauce
2 tbsp honey
1 tbsp vegetable oil
Thai Style
20 - 22 egg roll wraps
1/2 tsp Thai red chili paste, see appendix

2 tbsp lime juice
1 tbsp vegetable oil

Directions

1. Set your oven to 400 degrees F before doing anything else and line a baking sheet with the parchment paper.
2. For the teriyaki chips; in a bowl add the honey, teriyaki sauce and peanut oil and beat until combined nicely.
3. Cut each egg roll wrapper into 3 portions.
4. Coat each side of each wrapper portion with the honey mixture.
5. In the bottom of the prepared baking sheet, arrange the wontons.
6. Cook in the oven for about 15 minutes.
7. Remove from the oven and transfer the baking sheet onto a wire rack to crisp.
8. For the Thai chips; in a bowl, add the oil, lime juice and curry paste and beat until blended nicely.
9. Coat each side of each wrapper portion with the curry paste mixture.
10. In the bottom of the prepared baking sheet, arrange the wontons.
11. Cook in the oven for about 15 minutes.
12. Remove from the oven and transfer the baking sheet onto a wire rack to crisp.
13. Enjoy.

HAPPY WONTONS
with Orange Sauce

Prep Time: 25 mins
Total Time: 45 mins

Servings per Recipe: 1
Calories	52.6
Fat	1.3g
Cholesterol	12.3mg
Sodium	454.3mg
Carbohydrates	7.4g
Protein	2.7g

Ingredients

1 C. low sodium soy sauce
1/3 C. chopped cilantro
24 sprigs cilantro, leaves and tender stems
1 tbsp lemon zest
2 tbsp minced ginger
2 tsp minced ginger
2 tbsp toasted sesame oil
24 large shell-on shrimp
vegetable oil

24 square wonton wrappers
1/4 C. orange juice
3 tbsp lemon juice
2 tbsp orange marmalade
3 tbsp chopped green onions

Directions

1. In a bowl, add 1 tbsp of the sesame oil, 1/2 C. of the soy sauce, cilantro, 2 tbsp of the ginger and lemon zest and beat until well combined.
2. Add the shrimp and coat with the mixture generously.
3. Cover the bowl and keep aside for about 18-20 minutes.
4. In a colander, place the shrimp and keep aside until drained completely.
5. With the paper towels, pat dry the shrimp completely.
6. Place the cilantro and leaves stems in the center of each wonton wrapper evenly, followed by 1 shrimp lengthwise.
7. With wet fingers, moisten the edges of each wrapper and then, fold over the filling in a triangle shape.
8. Now, with your fingers, press the edges to seal completely.
9. In a deep skillet, add the oil and cook until its temperature reaches to 375 degrees F.
10. Add the wontons in batches and cook until golden brown from both sides.
11. With a slotted spoon, transfer the wontons onto a paper towel-lined plate to drain.
12. For the dipping sauce: in a bowl, add the remaining ingredients and mix until well combined.
13. Enjoy the wonton wrappers alongside the sauce.

Cucumber
Wontons

🥣 Prep Time: 5 mins
🕐 Total Time: 17 mins

Servings per Recipe: 1
Calories	37.0
Fat	0.7g
Cholesterol	0.7mg
Sodium	46.3mg
Carbohydrates	6.8g
Protein	0.9g

Ingredients

cooking spray
24 wonton wrappers
1 mango, peeled, pitted and diced
1 cucumber, peeled, seeded and diced
1/2 red onion, diced
2 tbsp fresh lime juice
2 tbsp chopped cilantro
1 tbsp olive oil

1 pinch cayenne pepper

Directions

1. Set your oven to 350 degrees F before doing anything else and grease the cups of the mini muffin pans.
2. Arrange 1 wonton wrapper in each prepared muffin cup and press to fit in a cup shape.
3. cook in the oven for about 9 - 12 minutes.
4. Remove from the oven and keep aside to cool completely.
5. Meanwhile, in a bowl, add the remaining ingredients and mix until well combined.
6. Fill each wonton cup with the salsa .
7. Enjoy.

CHIPOTLE WONTONS
with Southwest Salsa

Prep Time: 25 mins
Total Time: 40 mins

Servings per Recipe: 1
Calories	157.8
Fat	3.5g
Cholesterol	12.0mg
Sodium	287.5mg
Carbohydrates	25.7g
Protein	5.8g

Ingredients

Salsa
1/4 C. red onion, diced
1 large jalapeño, seeded and diced
2-3 green onions, diced
1/4 C. red bell pepper, diced
1/2 medium fresh pineapple, peeled, cored
and diced or
1 (20 oz.) cans pineapple chunks, drained
and diced
Filling
1/4 lb. cheddar cheese, shredded

1/4 lb. Monterey Jack cheese, shredded
3-4 long green chilies, roasted, peeled, seeded
and diced
1/2 tsp salt
1/4 tsp black pepper
1/4 tsp cumin
1-2 clove garlic, minced
24 egg roll wraps
flour
vegetable oil

Directions

1. For the salsa: in a bowl, add all the ingredients and mix well.
2. Cover the bowl and place in the fridge for about 4-6 hours.
3. In another bowl, add the cheeses, garlic, chile, cumin, salt and pepper and gently, toss to coat well.
4. Arrange the wonton wrappers onto a smooth surface.
5. Place about 1 tsp of the cheese mixture in the center of each wonton wrapper.
6. With wet fingers, moisten the edges of each wrapper and then, fold over the filling in a triangle shape.
7. Now, with your fingers, press the edges to seal completely.
8. Sprinkle each wonton with the flour.
9. In a deep skillet, add 3-inch of the oil and cook until its temperature reaches to 375 degrees F.
10. Add the wontons in batches and cook until golden brown from both sides.
11. With a slotted spoon, transfer the wontons onto a paper towel-lined plate to drain.
12. Enjoy warm.

Wonton
Ice Cream Sandwiches

Prep Time: 30 mins
Total Time: 30 mins

Servings per Recipe: 8
Calories   240.7
Fat   0.9g
Cholesterol   5.1mg
Sodium   357.3mg
Carbohydrates   52.4g
Protein   5.6g

Ingredients
1 (21 oz.) cans cinnamon apple pie filling
1 (16 oz.) packages wonton wrappers
oil
powdered sugar
ice cream

Directions
1. Place about 1 tbsp of the apple pie filling in the middle of each wonton wrapper.
2. Coat the edges of wrappers with wet fingers and fold them over the filling in a triangle shape.
3. With your fingers, press the edges to seal completely.
4. In a deep skillet, add 1/4-1/2-inch of the oil and cook until heated through.
5. Add the wontons in batches and cook until golden brown completely.
6. With a slotted spoon, transfer the wontons onto a paper towel-lined plate to drain.
7. Dust with the confectioners' sugar and enjoy.

CUPERTINO
Lunch Wontons

Prep Time: 15 mins
Total Time: 30 mins

Servings per Recipe: 24
Calories   35.4
Fat   0.1g
Cholesterol   0.7mg
Sodium   46.0mg
Carbohydrates   7.8g
Protein   0.8g

Ingredients
2 medium apples, McIntosh, peeled, cored
and minced
1 tbsp packed light brown sugar
1 tsp lemon juice
1/2 tsp ground cinnamon
24 wonton wrappers
1 1/2 tbsp powdered sugar

Directions
1. Set your oven to 350 degrees F before doing anything else and lightly grease a baking sheet.
2. In a bowl, add all the ingredients except the wonton wrappers and powdered sugar and mix until well combined.
3. Place the desired amount of the apple mixture in the center of each wonton wrapper.
4. With wet fingers, moisten the edges of each wrapper and then, fold over the filling in a triangle shape.
5. Now, with your fingers, press the edges to seal completely.
6. Spray each wonton with the cooking spray.
7. Cook in the oven for about 15 minutes.
8. Dust with the powdered sugar and enjoy.

Wonton Kyoto

🥣 Prep Time: 10 mins
🕐 Total Time: 14 mins

Servings per Recipe: 6
Calories	152.0
Fat	3.6g
Cholesterol	3.6mg
Sodium	423.3mg
Carbohydrates	24.8g
Protein	5.0g

Ingredients

1/4 C. sesame seeds
1/2 tsp garlic powder
1/2 tsp salt
1/2 tsp paprika
30 wonton wrappers, halved diagonally

Directions

1. Set your oven to 375 degrees F before doing anything else.
2. In a bowl, add all ingredients except the wrappers and mix until well combined.
3. In the bottom of a baking sheet, arrange the wontons and coat with the cooking spray.
4. Top each wonton with the sesame seeds mixture evenly.
5. Cook in the oven for about 4 minutes.
6. Enjoy warm.

ISLAND WONTONS
with Orange Sauce

Prep Time: 10 mins
Total Time: 30 mins

Servings per Recipe: 10
Calories	161.4
Fat	4.8g
Cholesterol	49.5mg
Sodium	749.7mg
Carbohydrates	21.8g
Protein	7.7g

Ingredients

Filling
1/2 lb. cooked shrimp, shelled, deveined and chopped into pieces
1 green onion, chopped fine
4 water chestnuts, chopped fine
1 egg white
1 tsp cornstarch
1/2 tsp salt
1/4 tsp black pepper
1 tsp soy sauce
1 tbsp oil
Island Dip
1/2 C. pineapple juice

1 green onion, sliced on the bias
1/2 C. peach halve in juice
2 tbsp orange marmalade
2 tbsp ketchup
2 tbsp rice vinegar
2 tbsp sugar
1 tsp salt
1/4 tsp dry mustard
2 drops hot sauce
Other
24 wonton wrappers
2 tbsp vegetable oil

Directions

1. For the filling: in a bowl, add all the ingredients and mix until well combined.
2. Place in the fridge for about 1 hour.
3. For the sauce: in a pan, add the green onion and pineapple juice and cook for about 2-4 minutes.
4. Meanwhile, in a blender, add the marmalade and peaches and pulse until chopped very finely.
5. In the pan, add the peach mixture with the remaining ingredients and cook until desired thickness, mixing often.
6. With a spoon place the filling mixture in the center of each wonton wrapper.
7. With wet fingers, moisten the edges of each wrapper and then, fold over the filling in a triangle shape.
8. Now, with your fingers, press the edges to seal completely.
9. In a skillet, add 2 tbsp of the oil over medium-low heat and cook until heated through.
10. Add the wontons in batches and cook for about 2-4 minutes, flipping once half way through.
11. With a slotted spoon, transfer the wontons onto a paper towel-lined plate to drain.
12. Enjoy alongside the sauce.

Corn Wonton Wraps

Prep Time: 1 hr
Total Time: 1 hr

Servings per Recipe: 8
Calories   113.7
Fat   0.3g
Cholesterol   0.0mg
Sodium   146.4mg
Carbohydrates   23.8g
Protein   3.2g

Ingredients
2 C. flour
1/2 tsp salt
1/2 C. warm water
cornstarch

Directions
1. In a bowl, add the flour and salt and mix well.
2. Then, sift the flour mixture into another bowl.
3. Slowly, add the warm water and mix until a stiff dough forms.
4. Place the dough onto a floured surface and with your hands, knead until dough becomes smooth.
5. With a kitchen towel, cover the dough and keep aside for about 15 minutes.
6. Divide the dough in 2 equal sized portions and roll the each portion into a thinner circle.
7. Prepare the wontons with your favorite filling and enjoy.

WONTON
World Cup

Prep Time: 20 mins
Total Time: 30 mins

Servings per Recipe: 24
Calories   35.5
Fat   0.1g
Cholesterol   0.8mg
Sodium   47.4mg
Carbohydrates   7.6g
Protein   1.0g

Ingredients
24 wonton wrappers
1 1/4 C. red grapes, halved
4-6 oz. low-fat vanilla yogurt
24 mandarin orange segments
mint leaf

Directions
1. Set your oven to 350 degrees F before doing anything else and grease cups of a mini muffin pan.
2. Place 1 wrapper into 1 of each prepared mini muffin cup and press to fit in a cup shape.
3. Cook in the oven for about 10 minutes.
4. Remove from the oven and keep aside to cool slightly.
5. Carefully, remove the wonton cups from the muffin pan and keep aside to cool completely.
6. In a bowl, add the yogurt and grapes and mix well.
7. Place the yogurt mixture into each wonton cup evenly.
8. Enjoy with a topping of the orange segment and mint leaves.

Expresso
Monday Wontons

🥣 Prep Time: 30 mins
🕐 Total Time: 43 mins

Servings per Recipe: 48
Calories	37.3
Fat	2.9g
Cholesterol	6.7mg
Sodium	5.4mg
Carbohydrates	2.7g
Protein	0.4g

Ingredients

1 tbsp whole wheat flour
1-17 1/3 oz. phyllo puff pastry sheet
1 (16 oz.) bags frozen pitted cherries, thawed
1/2 pint heavy whipping cream, whipped
1 (8 oz.) containers mascarpone cheese
1 tsp brewed espresso, cooled
1/2 tsp cinnamon

1/8 tsp nutmeg
2 tsp sugar
1/2 C. pecan pieces, divided
1/4 C. graham cracker, crushed into crumbs

Directions

1. Set your oven to 400 degrees F before doing anything else.
2. In a bowl, add the heavy whipping cream and with an electric beaters, beat until fluffy.
3. Add the mascarpone cheese chunks and beat until well combined.
4. In another bowl; add the coffee, sugar, nutmeg and cinnamon and mix until a paste is formed.
5. Add the coffee paste in to the bowl of the cream mixture and mix until well combined.
6. Add 1/4 C. of the pecan pieces and gently, stir to combine.
7. Add the graham cracker crumbs and gently, stir to combine.
8. Refrigerate before using.
9. Unfold 1 puff pastry sheet onto a floured wax paper.
10. With a floured rolling pin, roll the dough into a 12X12 inches circle.
11. With a knife, cut 24 squares from the dough pastry.
12. Repeat with the remaining puff pastry sheets.
13. Place 1 square into 1 of each mini muffin cup and press to fit in a cup shape.
14. In the bottom of each cup, place 1 cherry.
15. Cook in the oven for about 13 minutes.
16. Remove from the oven and keep aside to cool slightly.
17. Carefully, remove the wonton cups from the muffin pan and keep aside to cool for about 9-10 minutes.
18. Place the cream mixture in each wonton cup over the cherry.
19. Enjoy with a garnishing of the remaining pecan pieces.

5-INGREDIENT
Picnic Wontons

Prep Time: 20 mins
Total Time: 40 mins

Servings per Recipe: 6
Calories   255.1
Fat   13.8g
Cholesterol   44.4mg
Sodium   295.1mg
Carbohydrates   26.9g
Protein   6.2g

Ingredients
24 wonton wrappers
8 oz. cream cheese
1/4 C. powdered sugar
1 C. fresh raspberry
cinnamon sugar

Directions
1. In a food processor, add the raspberries, cream cheese and powdered sugar and pulse until smooth.
2. Place about 1 tsp of the raspberry mixture in the center of each wonton wrapper.
3. With wet fingers, moisten the edges of each wrapper and then, fold over the filling in a triangle shape.
4. Now, with your fingers, press the edges to seal completely.
5. In a deep skillet, add the oil and cook until heated through.
6. Add the wontons in batches and cook until golden brown from both sides.
7. With a slotted spoon, transfer the wontons onto a paper towel-lined plate to drain.
8. In a large skillet heat the oil till hot.
9. Dust with the cinnamon sugar and enjoy.

Taco
Wontons

Prep Time: 15 mins

Total Time: 33 mins

Servings per Recipe: 6

Calories	231.7
Fat	7.7g
Cholesterol	23.3mg
Sodium	441.0mg
Carbohydrates	25.3g
Protein	14.4g

Ingredients
cooking spray
2 tsp olive oil
1/2 lb. lean ground sirloin
2 oz. low-fat cheddar cheese
2 tbsp chopped green chilies, minced
1 tsp chili powder
1 tsp ground cumin
30 wonton wrappers

1/2 C. salsa

Directions
1. Set your oven to 350 degrees F before doing anything else grease a baking sheet.
2. In a skillet, add the oil over medium-high heat and cook until heated through.
3. Add the beef and cook for about 6-7 minutes.
4. Drain the grease from the skillet.
5. Stir in the chilies, cheese, cumin and chili powder and cook for about 1-2 minutes, mixing continuously.
6. Arrange the wonton wrappers onto a smooth surface.
7. Place desired amount of the mixture in the center of each wonton wrapper.
8. With wet fingers, moisten the edges of each wrapper and then, fold over the filling.
9. Now, with your fingers, press the edges to seal completely.
10. Now, gently twist ends of each to shape into firecracker.
11. In the bottom of the prepared baking sheet, arrange the wonton wrappers and spray each with the cooking spray.
12. Cook in the oven for about 15 minutes.
13. Enjoy alongside the salsa.

MOUNTAIN-GIRL
Wontons

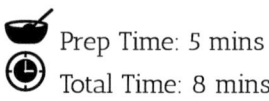

Prep Time: 5 mins
Total Time: 8 mins

Servings per Recipe: 10
Calories	183.9
Fat	12.1g
Cholesterol	55.0mg
Sodium	153.8mg
Carbohydrates	0.9g
Protein	17.0g

Ingredients
wonton wrapper
8 oz. goat cheese, chopped
4 chicken breasts, grilled and chopped
1 tsp basil, chopped
1/2 C. tomatoes, seeds removed and
chopped
oil

Directions
1. In a bowl, add the chicken, goat cheese, tomato and basil and mix well.
2. Place the desired amount of the mixture in the center of each wonton wrapper.
3. With wet fingers, moisten the edges of each wrapper and then, fold over the filling in a triangle shape.
4. Now, with your fingers, press the edges to seal completely.
5. In a deep skillet, add enough oil and cook until its temperature reaches to 350 degrees F.
6. Add the wontons in batches and cook until golden brown from both sides.
7. With a slotted spoon, transfer the wontons onto a paper towel-lined plate to drain.
8. Enjoy warm.

My First
Wontons

🥣 Prep Time: 5 mins
🕐 Total Time: 8 mins

Servings per Recipe: 1
Calories   41.4
Fat   1.5g
Cholesterol   0.7mg
Sodium   46.4mg
Carbohydrates   6.5g
Protein   1.1g

Ingredients

48 wonton wrappers
2 mashed bananas
8 oz. mascarpone cheese
1 C. chocolate, chopped

Directions

1. In a bowl, add the chocolate, cheese and bananas and mix well.
2. Place the desired amount of the mixture in the center of each wonton wrapper.
3. With wet fingers, moisten the edges of each wrapper and then, fold over the filling in a triangle shape.
4. Now, with your fingers, press the edges to seal completely.
5. In a deep skillet, add enough oil and cook until its temperature reaches to 350 degrees F.
6. Add the wontons in batches and cook for about 3 minutes.
7. With a slotted spoon, transfer the wontons onto a paper towel-lined plate to drain.
8. Enjoy warm.

COUNTRY
Wontons

Prep Time: 20 mins
Total Time: 25 mins

Servings per Recipe: 4
Calories   424.6
Fat   27.9g
Cholesterol   101.9mg
Sodium   758.1mg
Carbohydrates   36.3g
Protein   8.8g

Ingredients

6 oz. wonton wrappers
15 oz. canned pumpkin
1 large egg
1/4 tsp salt
1/4 tsp pepper
3 tbsp butter
3 tbsp olive oil
1 C. half-and-half cream
1 tsp rubbed sage
salt & pepper

Directions

1. In a bowl, add the egg, pumpkin, salt and pepper and mix well.
2. Place about 1- 1 1/2 tbsp of the mixture in the center of each wonton wrapper.
3. With wet fingers, moisten the edges of each wrapper and then, fold over the filling in a triangle shape.
4. Now, with your fingers, press the edges to seal completely.
5. In a pan, add the water and cook until boiling.
6. Add the stuffed raviolis and cook for about 3 minutes.
7. Drain the raviolis well.
8. In a pan, add the oil and butter and cook until heated through.
9. Add the sage, half-and-half, salt and pepper and stir to combine well.
10. Carefully, place the raviolis and cook for about 1-2 minutes.
11. Enjoy hot.

Arizona
Wontons

Prep Time: 5 mins
Total Time: 10 mins

Servings per Recipe: 4
Calories   297.2
Fat   13.4g
Cholesterol   48.6mg
Sodium   463.6mg
Carbohydrates   39.2g
Protein   4.9g

Ingredients

12 store-bought wonton wrappers
1 egg
1 tbsp water
6 jalapeño Jack cheese, snacks halved
1 green onion, chopped
3 tbsp vegetable oil
1 tbsp sesame seeds
3/4 C. plum sauce

Directions

1. In a bowl, add the water and egg and beat well.
2. Arrange the wonton wrappers onto a smooth surface.
3. Coat the edges of each wrapper with the egg wash.
4. Arrange 1 cheese piece in the center of each wonton wrapper horizontally, followed by the green onions.
5. Fold the sides of the wrapper over the filling and roll like a cylinder.
6. In a deep skillet, add the oil over medium-high heat and cook until heated through.
7. Cook for about 3-5 minutes, flipping often.
8. With a slotted spoon, transfer the wontons onto a paper towel-lined plate to drain.
9. Transfer the wontons onto a platter and
10. sprinkle with the sesame seeds.
11. Enjoy alongside the plum sauce.

ASIAN
Salad Crisps

Prep Time: 10 mins
Total Time: 15 mins

Servings per Recipe: 5
Calories	146.8
Fat	11.5g
Cholesterol	1.4mg
Sodium	91.5mg
Carbohydrates	9.2g
Protein	1.5g

Ingredients
10 wonton wrappers, cut into strips
2 oz. peanut oil

Directions
1. In a deep skillet, add 1-inch of the oil over medium-high heat and cook until its temperature reaches to 360 degrees F.
2. Add the strips in batches and cook until golden brown from both sides.
3. With a slotted spoon, transfer the fried strips onto a paper towel-lined plate to drain.
4. Enjoy.

Ballpark
Wontons

Prep Time: 30 mins
Total Time: 50 mins

Servings per Recipe: 1
Calories	40.2
Fat	1.1g
Cholesterol	9.5mg
Sodium	49.3mg
Carbohydrates	6.1g
Protein	1.3g

Ingredients

Filling
2 tbsp packed brown sugar
2 tbsp unsweetened dried shredded coconut
2 tbsp chopped unsalted dry roasted peanuts
2 tbsp sesame seeds
Wonton

24 wonton wrappers
24 mint leaves
1 egg, lightly beaten
cooking oil

Directions

1. In a bowl, add the peanuts, coconut, brown sugar and sesame seeds and mix well.
2. Place 1 tsp of the peanut mixture in the middle of each wrapper and top each with a mint leaf.
3. With wet fingers, moisten the edges of each wrapper and then, fold over the filling in a triangle shape.
4. Now, with your fingers, press the edges to seal completely.
5. In a deep skillet, add the oil and cook until its temperature reaches to 350 degrees F.
6. Add the wontons in batches and cook until golden brown from both sides.
7. With a slotted spoon, transfer the wontons onto a paper towel-lined plate to drain.
8. Enjoy warm.

ORIENTAL
Garden Chips

Prep Time: 10 mins
Total Time: 20 mins

Servings per Recipe: 2
Calories   116.6
Fat   0.9g
Cholesterol   3.4mg
Sodium   291.3mg
Carbohydrates   21.5g
Protein   4.9g

Ingredients
8 wonton wrappers
2 tbsp fat-free margarine, melted
Splenda sugar substitute
cinnamon
1/4 C. nonfat plain yogurt
2 tbsp sugar-free strawberry jam
liquid stevia

Directions
1. Set your oven to 350 degrees F before doing anything else and grease a baking sheet.
2. In the bottom of the prepared baking sheet, arrange the wonton wrappers.
3. Coat each wrapper with the margarine and dust with the splenda and cinnamon.
4. Cook in the oven for about 8 minutes.
5. Meanwhile, in a bowl, add the strawberry preserves, yogurt, Splenda and 1-2 drops of liquid stevia and mix well.
6. Remove the wonton wrappers from the oven and then, break each into desired sized chips.
7. Enjoy the wonton chips alongside the yogurt mixture.

Picnic
Coleslaw Wontons

🥣 Prep Time: 25 mins
🕐 Total Time: 40 mins

Servings per Recipe: 4	
Calories	78.0
Fat	0.3g
Cholesterol	2.1mg
Sodium	391.9mg
Carbohydrates	15.4g
Protein	3.1g

Ingredients
1 C. coleslaw mix
1 inch ginger, grated
1 clove garlic, mashed
1 tbsp soy sauce
2 tsp chili oil
salt
ground pepper
12 wonton wrappers

Directions
1. In a skillet, add 1 tsp of the oil over high heat and cook until heated through.
2. Add the garlic and ginger and sauté for about 15 seconds.
3. Stir in the coleslaw mix and sauté for about 1 minute.
4. Add the chili oil, soy sauce, salt and pepper and stir to combine.
5. Remove from the heat and keep aside to cool.
6. Place 1 tsp of the coleslaw mixture in the center of each wrapper.
7. With wet fingers, moisten the edges of each wrapper and then, fold over the filling in a triangle shape.
8. Now, with your fingers, press the edges to seal completely.
9. In a steamer, and the wontons in batches and steam for about 15 minutes.
10. Enjoy hot alongside your favorite sauce.

NTON
Juffalo Style

Prep Time: 30 mins
Total Time: 38 mins

Servings per Recipe: 4
Calories   351.0
Fat   26.5g
Cholesterol   77.8mg
Sodium   686.0mg
Carbohydrates   2.5g
Protein   25.2g

Ingredients
1 lb. chicken breast, season with salt and
pepper
3 tbsp Frank's hot sauce
1/2 C. chunky blue cheese dressing
1 tsp chopped onion
1/2 package store-bought wonton

Directions
1. Set your oven to 450 degrees F before doing anything else.
2. Heat a greased skillet and cook the chicken breast until cooked through.
3. Remove from the heat and cut each chicken breast into small chunks.
4. In a bowl, add the breast chunks and remaining ingredients except the wonton skins and mix until well combined.
5. Place 1 wrapper into 1 of lightly greased mini muffin cup and press to fit in a cup shape.
6. Place 1 tsp of the chicken mixture into each wonton cup and then, fold the corners tightly.
7. Cook in the oven for about 7-8 minutes.
8. Enjoy warm.

Wontons
Alaska

🥣 Prep Time: 40 mins

🕐 Total Time: 60 mins

Servings per Recipe: 30
Calories	10.3
Fat	0.2g
Cholesterol	3.6mg
Sodium	56.0mg
Carbohydrates	0.4g
Protein	1.5g

Ingredients

1 (7 1/2 oz.) cans salmon, skin and bones removed
1/4 C. shredded carrot
4 scallions, chopped
1/2 C. alfalfa sprout
1 1/2 tbsp soy sauce
2 tsp grated gingerroot
2 garlic cloves, crushed

about 30 wonton wrapper
oil

Directions

1. In a bowl, add the salmon, sprouts, carrot, scallions, garlic, ginger and soy sauce and toss to coat well.
2. Place 1 tsp of the salmon mixture in the center of each wonton wrapper.
3. With wet fingers, moisten the edges of each wrapper and then, fold over the filling in a triangle shape.
4. In a deep skillet, add the oil over medium-high heat and cook until heated through.
5. Add the wontons in batches and cook for about 6-8 minutes, flipping once half way through.
6. With a slotted spoon, transfer the wontons onto a paper towel-lined plate to drain.
7. Enjoy hot alongside your favorite dipping sauce.

WONTONS
Winnipeg

Prep Time: 10 mins
Total Time: 35 mins

Servings per Recipe: 1
Calories	51.1
Fat	2.5g
Cholesterol	19.2mg
Sodium	59.2mg
Carbohydrates	5.5g
Protein	1.4g

Ingredients
Filling
1 C. cooked pumpkin
8 oz. cream cheese, softened
1/4 C. firmly packed brown sugar
1/4 tsp vanilla extract
1/8 tsp cinnamon
1 pinch nutmeg
1 large egg, beaten
Wrapper
1 (8 oz.) packages wonton wrappers
1 egg, beaten
oil
powdered sugar

caramel sauce, thinned with water

Directions
1. For the filling: in a bowl, add all the ingredients and beat until well combined.
2. Arrange the wonton wrappers onto a smooth surface.
3. With beaten egg, coat 1-inch wide edge.
4. Place 1 tbsp of the filling mixture in the center of each wrapper.
5. Fold each wonton in half over the filling in a triangle shape.
6. Now, with your fingers, press the edges to seal completely.
7. Coat the outside of each wonton wrapper with the beaten egg.
8. In a deep skillet, add about 1-inch of the oil and cook until heated through.
9. Add the wontons in batches and cook until golden brown from both sides.
10. With a slotted spoon, transfer the wontons onto a paper towel-lined plate to drain.
11. Dust with the powdered sugar and drizzle with the caramel sauce.
12. Enjoy.

Wonton Salad 101

Prep Time: 15 mins
Total Time: 15 mins

Servings per Recipe: 2
Calories	1060.3
Fat	55.8g
Cholesterol	10.2mg
Sodium	2540.1mg
Carbohydrates	119.9g
Protein	30.4g

Ingredients

Salad
2 heads chopped romaine lettuce
2 C. diced boneless skinless chicken breasts
1/2 C. diced spring onion
3/4 C. lightly chopped cashews
1/2 tbsp sesame seeds
1 (8 oz.) packages wonton wrappers, sliced in 1/2 fried and salted

Dressing
3 tbsp rice vinegar
2 tbsp sugar
3 tbsp soy sauce
2 dashes garlic powder
1/4 C. oil

Directions

1. For the salad: in a bowl, add all the ingredients and mix well.

2. For the dressing: in a bowl, add all the ingredients and beat until well combined.

3. Pour the dressing over the salad and toss to coat well.

4. Enjoy.

OPEN FACE
Wontons

Prep Time: 15 mins
Total Time: 25 mins

Servings per Recipe: 1
Calories   27.0
Fat   1.8g
Cholesterol   13.0mg
Sodium   67.5mg
Carbohydrates   0.1g
Protein   2.3g

Ingredients
1 lb. ground beef
1 large egg
1 tsp ground ginger
3 garlic cloves, minced
1/4 C. scallion, chopped
1/4 tsp cayenne pepper
1 tsp salt
1/2 tsp ground black pepper
oil

Directions
1. In a bowl, add all the ingredients except the oil and mix until blended nicely.
2. In a deep skillet, add the oil and cook until its temperature reaches to 375 degrees F.
3. With a tsp, place the beef mixture in small batches and cook until desired doneness.
4. With a slotted spoon, transfer the beef wontons onto a paper towel-lined plate to drain.
5. Enjoy alongside your favorite dipping sauce.

Wonton
Ice Cream

Prep Time: 25 mins
Total Time: 35 mins

Servings per Recipe: 24
Calories	77.6
Fat	2.9g
Cholesterol	5.8mg
Sodium	90.6mg
Carbohydrates	11.4g
Protein	1.7g

Ingredients
24 wonton wrappers
butter-flavored cooking spray
1 tbsp sugar, divided
1/4 C. sugar, divided
1 tsp cinnamon
1 (8 oz.) packages reduced-fat cream cheese
1 tsp vanilla

1/4 C. semi-sweet chocolate chips
1/4 C. chopped pecans
24 maraschino cherries, with stems

Directions
1. Set your oven to 350 degrees F before doing anything else and lightly, grease cups of the mini muffin pans.
2. Arrange the wonton wrappers onto a smooth surface.
3. In a bowl, add 1 tbsp of the sugar and cinnamon and mix well.
4. Spray each wonton wrapper with the butter flavored spray and then dust each with cinnamon sugar.
5. Place 1 wrapper into 1 of each prepared mini muffin cup and press to fit in a cup shape.
6. Cook in the oven for about 4-5 minutes.
7. Remove from the oven and immediately, transfer the wonton cups onto an ungreased baking sheet.
8. Cook in the oven for about 2-3 minutes.
9. Remove from the oven and place the wonton cups onto a wire rack.
10. In a bowl, add the remaining sugar, cream cheese and vanilla and beat until smooth.
11. Add the pecans and chocolate chips and gently stir to combine.
12. Place the mixture into each wonton cup evenly and enjoy with a garnishing of the cherries.

WONTONS
Mexico

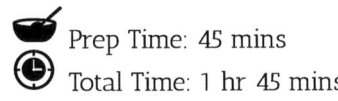 Prep Time: 45 mins

Total Time: 1 hr 45 mins

Servings per Recipe: 1
Calories	84.6
Fat	4.7g
Cholesterol	14.2mg
Sodium	127.9mg
Carbohydrates	5.8g
Protein	4.7g

Ingredients
30 wonton wrappers
8 whole green chilies, canned, seeds
removed and cut into strips
1 lb. Monterey Jack cheese, cut into strips
oil

Directions
1. Place 1 chile strip in the center of each wonton wrapper, followed by the cheese strip.
2. With wet fingers, moisten the edges of each wrapper and then, fold over the filling in a triangle shape.
3. Now, with your fingers, press the edges to seal completely.
4. Keep aside for about 4-5 minutes.
5. In a deep skillet, add the oil and cook until heated through.
6. Add the wontons in batches and cook until golden brown completely.
7. With a slotted spoon, transfer the wontons onto a paper towel-lined plate to drain.
8. Enjoy warm.

Jamaica

🥣 Prep Time: 30 mins
🕐 Total Time: 50 mins

Servings per Recipe: 30
Calories   83.7
Fat   3.0g
Cholesterol   4.5mg
Sodium   101.0mg
Carbohydrates   12.3g
Protein   1.9g

Ingredients

1 C. shrimp, cooked and chopped
1 C. unsweetened flaked coconut
1 (3 oz.) packages cream cheese, softened
1 (9 3/4 oz.) jars seafood cocktail sauce, divided
60 wonton wrappers
vegetable oil
1/4 C. honey

Directions

1. In a bowl, add the shrimp, 1/2 C. of the shrimp sauce, cream cheese and coconut and mix well.
2. Place about 1 tbsp of the mixture in the center of each wonton wrapper.
3. With wet fingers, moisten the edges of each wrapper and then, fold over the filling in a triangle shape.
4. Now, with your fingers, press the edges to seal completely.
5. Place about 2 tsp of the shrimp mixture onto 1 corner of each wonton wrapper.
6. With wet fingers, moisten the edges of each wrapper and then, fold over the filling in a triangle shape.
7. Now, with your fingers, press the edges to seal completely.
8. In a deep skillet, add the 1/4-inch deep oil over medium-high heat and cook for about 1 minute, flipping once half way through.
9. Add the wontons in batches and cook until golden brown from both sides.
10. With a slotted spoon, transfer the wontons onto a paper towel-lined plate to drain.
11. Meanwhile, in a bowl, add the honey and remaining cocktail sauce and mix well.
12. Enjoy the wontons alongside the sauce.

HONG KONG
Wonton Soup

🥣 Prep Time: 40 mins
🕐 Total Time: 1 hr

Servings per Recipe: 4
Calories   333.5
Fat   6.1g
Cholesterol   99.0mg
Sodium   2678.6mg
Carbohydrates   47.0g
Protein   21.8g

Ingredients
Wonton
32 wonton wrappers
1 tsp crushed garlic
2 tsp crushed ginger
1 tsp sesame oil
3 tsp soy sauce
150 g ground chicken
32 shrimp
2 spring onions, chopped
Soup
5 C. water
6 tsp instant chicken bouillon granules
1 spring onion

1 onion, sliced
2 carrots
1/2 tsp chili powder
1 spring onion, sliced and soaked in ice water

Directions
1. For the soup: in a pan, add all the ingredients and cook until boiling.
2. Reduce the heat to keep the soup hot.
3. Meanwhile, in a bowl, add the ground chicken, garlic, ginger, sesame oil and soy sauce and mix until well combined.
4. Place about 1 tsp of the mixture in the center of each wonton wrapper, followed by 1 shrimp.
5. With wet fingers, moisten the edges of each wrapper and then, fold upwards to create a parcel.
6. In a pan of the boiling water, add the wontons in batches and cook for about 5 minutes.
7. With a slotted spoon, transfer the wontons into serving bowls.
8. Remove the spring onion slices from the ice water and divide into bowls with the wontons.
9. Place the hot soup on top and enjoy.

Wonton
Clam Salad

🍲 Prep Time: 10 mins
🕐 Total Time: 22 mins

Servings per Recipe: 4
Calories	990.3
Fat	35.8g
Cholesterol	164.1mg
Sodium	1033.3mg
Carbohydrates	124.8g
Protein	40.3g

Ingredients

1 (14 oz.) packages wonton skins
1 (12 oz.) packages cream cheese, softened
2 (6 1/2 oz.) cans minced clams, drained
1/4 C. green onion, chopped
1/2 tsp soy sauce
3 drops sesame oil
2 tsp fresh ginger, grated
1 C. pineapple jam

1 tbsp hot mustard
1 tbsp honey, heated

Directions

1. Set your oven to 425 degrees F before doing anything else and grease a baking sheet.
2. In a bowl, add the clams, cream cheese, green onion, 1 tsp of the ginger, soy sauce and sesame oil and mix until well combined.
3. carefully, unwrap the wonton skins.
4. Place about 1 tsp of the mixture in the center of each wonton wrapper.
5. With wet fingers, moisten the edges of each wrapper and then, fold over the filling in a triangle shape.
6. Now, with your fingers, press the edges to seal completely.
7. In the bottom of the prepared baking sheet, arrange the wonton wrappers.
8. Cook in the oven for about 12 minutes.
9. Meanwhile, for the dipping sauce: in a bowl, add the honey, mustard, jam and remaining ginger and mix until well combined.
10. Enjoy the wontons alongside the dipping sauce.

SALAD WONTON
Lunch Box

Prep Time: 10 mins
Total Time: 20 mins

Servings per Recipe: 4
Calories   190.6
Fat   4.1g
Cholesterol   3.6mg
Sodium   231.9mg
Carbohydrates   34.0g
Protein   4.9g

Ingredients
20 pieces wonton wrappers, cut into strips
1 small cucumber, sliced
1 tomatoes, sliced
1 orange, juiced and grated, divided
2 tbsp rice vinegar
1 tbsp olive oil
1 tbsp sugar

Directions
1. In a pan of the boiling water, cook the wonton strips until desired doneness.
2. Drain the wonton strips and immediately, place into a bowl of the cold water.
3. Drain well.
4. For the dressing: in a bowl, add the sugar, oil, vinegar and orange juice and beat until well combined.
5. In a another bowl, add the wonton strips, tomato and cucumber and mix.
6. Pour the dressing and toss to coat well.
7. Enjoy with a garnishing of 1 tbsp of the orange peel.

Candy Wontons with Styles

Prep Time: 40 mins
Total Time: 45 mins

Servings per Recipe: 10
Calories	55.5
Fat	2.5g
Cholesterol	5.8mg
Sodium	13.4mg
Carbohydrates	7.6g
Protein	0.9g

Ingredients

Wrapper
1 1/2 C. flour
1 egg, beaten
1 pinch salt
Sweet Filling Style 1
1 C. shredded coconut
1/4 C. coconut syrup
1 tsp grated lemon rind
Sweet Filling Style 2
1/2 C. chopped macadamia nuts
1 tbsp chopped candied ginger
1 tbsp lemon juice
1 tbsp dark brown sugar
Sweet Filling Style 3
1/2 C. sliced dried banana
1 tbsp chopped candied ginger
1 tbsp lemon juice
1 tbsp honey
powdered sugar

Directions

1. In a bowl, add the egg, flour and salt and mix well.
2. Add enough water and mix until a stiff dough forms.
3. Place the dough onto a lightly floured surface and with your hands, knead for about 10 minutes.
4. With a kitchen towel, cover the dough for about 10 minutes.
5. Meanwhile, for the filling: in a bowl, add all the ingredients and mix until well combined.
6. Now, with a floured rolling pin, roll the dough into a very thin circle.
7. Cut 3-inch squares from the dough.
8. Place about 1 tbsp of the mixture in the center of each wonton wrapper.
9. Roll each square tightly around the filling and then, twist the ends like a candy wrapper.
10. In a deep skillet, add the oil and cook until its temperature reaches to 375 degrees F.
11. Add the wontons in batches and cook for about 5 minutes.
12. With a slotted spoon, transfer the wontons onto a paper towel-lined plate to drain.
13. Dust with the powdered sugar and enjoy.

WONTONS
Mediterranean

Prep Time: 15 mins
Total Time: 30 mins

Servings per Recipe: 6
Calories   1306.5
Fat   127.9 g
Cholesterol   37.2mg
Sodium   1111.6mg
Carbohydrates   29.7 g
Protein   14.5 g

Ingredients
2 tbsp margarine
2 tbsp onions, minced
1/2 tsp garlic, minced
1 (8 oz.) packages shredded Colby-
Monterey Jack cheese
1 (6 oz.) cans black pitted ripe olives, well
drained and chopped
30 wonton wrappers
3-6 C. oil

2 tsp seasoning salt
1 1/2 C. salsa

Directions
1. In a large skillet, add the margarine and cook until melted.
2. Add the onion and stir fry for about 4 minutes.
3. Add the garlic and stir fry for about 1 minute.
4. Set the heat to low and add the cheese, stirring continuously until just melted.
5. Remove from the heat and stir in the olives.
6. Keep aside to cool.
7. Place about 1 tsp of the mixture in the center of each wonton wrapper.
8. With wet fingers, moisten the edges of each wrapper and then, fold over the filling in a triangle shape.
9. Now, with your fingers, press the edges to seal completely.
10. In a deep skillet, add the oil and cook until heated through.
11. Add the wontons in batches and cook until golden brown from both sides.
12. With a slotted spoon, transfer the wontons onto a paper towel-lined plate to drain.
13. Enjoy with a sprinkling of the seasoned salt alongside the salsa.

Glazed
Szechuan Wontons

🥣 Prep Time: 50 mins
🕐 Total Time: 1 hr 40 mins

Servings per Recipe: 40
Calories	39.0
Fat	0.6g
Cholesterol	5.6mg
Sodium	134.1mg
Carbohydrates	6.4g
Protein	1.8g

Ingredients

1/2 lb. ground chicken
2 tbsp minced onions
2 garlic cloves, crushed
2 tsp minced ginger
1 tbsp soy sauce
40 wonton wrappers
Szechuan
1 C. raspberries, unsweetened
2 tbsp vinegar
2 tbsp sugar

1/2 tsp hot chili sauce
1 1/2 tsp grated ginger
2 garlic cloves, crushed
1 tbsp lime juice
1 tbsp liquid honey
1 tsp salt
1 tbsp cornstarch
1 tbsp water

Directions

1. Set your oven to 400 degrees F before doing anything else and line a baking sheet with the parchment paper.
2. In a skillet, add the oil over medium heat and cook until heated.
3. Add the ground chicken, onions, cloves, ginger and soy sauce and cook until done completely.
4. Remove from the heat and keep aside to cool.
5. Place about 1 tsp of the mixture in the center of each wonton wrapper.
6. With wet fingers, moisten the edges of each wrapper and then, fold over the filling in a triangle shape.
7. Now, with your fingers, press the edges to seal completely.
8. In the bottom of the prepared baking sheet, arrange the wonton wrappers and coat each with the oil slightly.
9. Cook in the oven for about 20-30 minutes.
10. Meanwhile, for the sauce: in a food processor, add the raspberries and pulse until pureed.
11. Through a sieve, strain the blueberry puree by pressing with a spatula.
12. In a pot, add he blueberry puree, 2 garlic cloves, 1 1/2 tsp grated ginger, sugar, honey, vinegar, hot chili sauce, lime juice and salt and cook until boiling, mixing occasionally.
13. In a bowl, add the cornstarch and 1 tbsp of the water and mix well.
14. Add the cornstarch mixture into the pan, mixing continuously.
15. Cook until desired thickness of the sauce.
16. Enjoy the wontons alongside the warm sauce.

WONTONS
Idaho

Prep Time: 10 mins
Total Time: 20 mins

Servings per Recipe: 1
Calories	68.3
Fat	3.0g
Cholesterol	7.8mg
Sodium	178.7mg
Carbohydrates	7.1g
Protein	3.0g

Ingredients
1/2 C. mashed potatoes
1 1/2 tsp onion powder
2 tsp garlic powder
1/2 tsp cayenne powder
1/2 tsp ground black pepper
2 tbsp mayonnaise
2 chopped green onions
1/2 C. mozzarella cheese
6 slices crisp cooked bacon, crumbled

15 wonton wrappers
oil

Directions
1. In a bowl, add the mayonnaise, cheese, mashed potato, onion, garlic, green onions, cayenne powder and black pepper and mix until well combined.
2. Add the bacon and gently, stir to combine.
3. Place about 1 tbsp of the mixture in the center of each wonton wrapper.
4. With wet fingers, moisten the edges of each wrapper and then, fold over the filling in a triangle shape.
5. Now, with your fingers, press the edges to seal completely.
6. In a deep skillet, add the oil and cook until heated through.
7. Add the wontons in batches and cook until golden brown from both sides.
8. With a slotted spoon, transfer the wontons onto a paper towel-lined plate to drain.
9. Enjoy warm.

Karen's
Hot Tofu Wontons

🍳 Prep Time: 10 mins
🕐 Total Time: 20 mins

Servings per Recipe: 1
Calories	41.4
Fat	0.5g
Cholesterol	0.7mg
Sodium	221.9mg
Carbohydrates	6.9g
Protein	2.1g

Ingredients
24 wonton wrappers
1 (12 oz.) boxes firm silken tofu, drained
6 button mushrooms
1 (4 oz.) cans water chestnuts
1/4 C. chili sauce
1/2 tsp salt
2 garlic cloves
2 tbsp soy sauce
1 tbsp spicy mustard

Directions
1. Set your oven to 375 degrees F before doing anything else and grease a baking sheet.
2. In a blender, add the tofu, chestnuts, mushrooms and garlic and pulse until a slightly chunky mixture is formed.
3. Transfer the mixture into a bowl with the mustard, chili sauce, soy sauce and salt and mix well.
4. Place about 1 tsp of the mixture in the center of each wonton wrapper.
5. With wet fingers, moisten the edges of each wrapper and then, fold over the filling in a triangle shape.
6. Now, with your fingers, press the edges to seal completely.
7. In the bottom of the prepared baking sheet, arrange the wonton wrappers.
8. Cook in the oven for about 10 minutes.
9. Enjoy the wontons alongside your favorite sauce.

HOT TUNA
Wontons in Japan

Prep Time: 20 mins
Total Time: 40 mins

Servings per Recipe: 1

Calories	87.2
Fat	4.8g
Cholesterol	5.0mg
Sodium	216.0mg
Carbohydrates	6.5g
Protein	4.6g

Ingredients
Wonton
1/2 C. sesame oil
40 wonton skins
Filling
1 lb. frozen soybeans
1 tbsp wasabi powder
1 tsp sea salt
1 lemon, juice
6 tbsp water

2 tbsp canola oil
Spicy Tuna
1/2 C. low sodium soy sauce
2 tbsp sake
2 tbsp light brown sugar
1 tsp red chili paste, see appendix
1 lb. sushi-quality tuna, cut into strips
2 tbsp sesame seeds, toasted

Directions

1. Set your oven to 350 degrees F before doing anything else and grease 2 baking sheets with the sesame oil.
2. In the bottom of the prepared baking sheet, arrange the wonton wrappers and coat each with the sesame oil.
3. Cook in the oven for about 15 minutes.
4. Remove from the oven and with a spatula, transfer the wonton crisps onto a platter.
5. Keep aside to cool.
6. In a pan, add the water and cook until boiling.
7. Add the soy beans and cook for about 5 minutes.
8. Drain the soy beans well and then, remove the beans from their pods.
9. In a blender, add the beans, wasabi, lemon juice, water and salt and pulse until pureed.
10. Add the canola oil and pulse until smooth.
11. Place in the fridge until using.
12. In a bowl, add the sake, brown sugar, soy sauce and chili paste and beat until the sugar is dissolved completely.
13. In the bottom of a shallow dish, place the tuna strips in a single layer.
14. Place the marinade over the tuna evenly.
15. Cover the dish and place in the fridge for about 20 minutes.
16. Place a spoonful of the edamame puree onto each wonton crisp, followed by a tuna slice.
17. Enjoy with a garnishing of the sesame seeds.

Fall
Wonton Platter

Prep Time: 15 mins
Total Time: 21 mins

Servings per Recipe: 50
Calories	43.9
Fat	0.9g
Cholesterol	3.2mg
Sodium	53.5mg
Carbohydrates	8.0g
Protein	1.0g

Ingredients
1/2 C. cream cheese, softened
1 C. sun-dried cranberries, chopped
5-6 peeled and diced apples
16 oz. baked pumpkin puree
50 wonton wrappers
brown sugar
cinnamon
oil

Directions
1. In a bowl, add the apple, cranberry and pumpkin puree and mix well.
2. Arrange the wonton wrappers onto a smooth surface.
3. Place some of the cream cheese in the center of each wrapper, followed by the apple mixture, cinnamon and brown sugar.
4. Place about 1 tbsp of the mixture in the center of each wonton wrapper.
5. With wet fingers, moisten the edges of each wrapper and then, fold over the filling in a triangle shape.
6. Now, with your fingers, press the edges to seal completely.
7. In a deep skillet, add the oil and cook until its temperature reaches to 350 degrees F.
8. Add the wontons in batches and cook for about 5-6 minutes, flipping once half way through.
9. With a slotted spoon, transfer the wontons onto a paper towel-lined plate to drain.
10. Enjoy alongside your favorite sauce.

WONTONS
Kerala

Prep Time: 15 mins
Total Time: 25 mins

Servings per Recipe: 1
Calories   66.2
Fat   4.2g
Cholesterol   22.5mg
Sodium   82.4mg
Carbohydrates   4.9g
Protein   1.9g

Ingredients

oil
1 (8 oz.) packages cream cheese, cubed
20 wonton wrappers
5 tsp chopped scallions, both white and
green parts
curry powder
1 whole egg, beaten
sweet and sour sauce, or duck sauce

Directions

1. Set your oven to 350 degrees F before doing anything else.
2. Arrange a cream cheese cube in the center of each wonton wrapper, followed by the scallion and a little curry powder evenly.
3. Coat the sides of each wrapper with the beaten egg and fold over the filling in a triangle shape.
4. Now, with your fingers, press the edges to seal completely.
5. In a deep skillet, add the oil and cook until heated through.
6. Add the wontons in batches and cook until golden brown from both sides.
7. With a slotted spoon, transfer the wontons onto a paper towel-lined plate to drain.
8. Enjoy hot alongside the sweet and sour sauce.

Fruit Fantasy
Wontons

🍳 Prep Time: 5 mins
🕐 Total Time: 5 mins

Servings per Recipe: 6
Calories	289.3
Fat	15.8g
Cholesterol	49.6mg
Sodium	301.6mg
Carbohydrates	26.6g
Protein	11.9g

Ingredients
peanut oil
1 packet wonton skins
2 apples, peeled, cored and cut into small
pieces
10 oz. sharp cheddar cheese, cubed
Toppings
1/2 C. brown sugar
2 tbsp ground cinnamon

Directions
1. In a bowl, add the cinnamon and brown sugar and mix well.
2. Place an apple piece in the center of each wrapper, followed by 1 cheddar cheese cube.
3. With wet fingers, moisten the edges of each wrapper and then, fold over the filling in a triangle shape.
4. Now, with your fingers, press the edges to seal completely.
5. In a deep skillet, add the oil and cook until heated through.
6. Add the wontons in batches and cook until golden brown from both sides.
7. With a slotted spoon, transfer the wontons onto a paper towel-lined plate to drain.
8. Dredge the wontons with the with the cinnamon sugar and enjoy.

COUNTRY SWEET
Layered Wontons (Napoleons)

Prep Time: 15 mins
Total Time: 25 mins

Servings per Recipe: 8
Calories   251.2
Fat   10.3g
Cholesterol   33.4mg
Sodium   229.9mg
Carbohydrates   36.9g
Protein   4.6g

Ingredients
Wontons
1/4 C. honey
24 refrigerated wonton wrappers
Filling
1 (8 oz.) containers cream cheese
2 tbsp honey
1/2 tsp vanilla extract
Fruit
1 pint strawberry, hulled, sliced

1 pint blueberries

Directions
1. Set your oven to 400 degrees F before doing anything else and line 2 baking sheets with pieces of foil.
2. In a microwave-safe bowl, add the honey and microwave for about 25 seconds.
3. Coat one side of each wonton wrapper with the honey evenly.
4. In the bottom of the prepared baking sheet, arrange the wonton wrappers, honey side up.
5. Cook in the oven for about 7 minutes.
6. Remove from the oven an place onto a wire rack.
7. For the filling: in a bowl, add the honey, cream cheese and vanilla and beat until smooth.
8. Place about 1 tbsp of the filling onto 1 wrapper evenly, followed by the
9. strawberry slices.
10. Cover with another wonton wrapper.
11. Place another tbsp of the filling onto second wrapper evenly, followed by the blueberries.
12. Now, cover with a third wonton wrapper and
13. Repeat with the remaining wrappers, filling and berries.
14. Enjoy with a garnishing of the strawberries and blueberries.

Garden Party
Wontons

Prep Time: 20 mins
Total Time: 26 mins

Servings per Recipe: 12
Calories	100.2
Fat	4.4g
Cholesterol	6.5mg
Sodium	108.4mg
Carbohydrates	13.4g
Protein	1.5g

Ingredients
24 wonton wrappers
12 large chocolate coins, unwrapped
2 tbsp butter
2 tbsp canola oil
1/4 C. cinnamon sugar

Directions
1. Arrange 12 wonton wrappers onto a smooth surface.
2. Place 1 chocolate coin in the center of each wonton wrapper.
3. With wet fingers, moisten the edges of each wrapper and then, fold over the filling in a triangle shape.
4. Now, with your fingers, press the edges to seal completely.
5. In a deep skillet, add the oil and butter over medium heat and cook until heated through.
6. Add the wontons in batches and cook for about 4-6 minutes, flipping once half way through.
7. With a slotted spoon, transfer the wontons onto a paper towel-lined plate to drain.
8. Coat each wonton with the cinnamon sugar and enjoy warm.

ZARA'S
Sweet Wontons

Prep Time: 15 mins
Total Time: 30 mins

Servings per Recipe: 6
Calories   104.0
Fat   1.9g
Cholesterol   1.5mg
Sodium   111.1mg
Carbohydrates   19.5g
Protein   2.3g

Ingredients
1 small ripe banana, mashed
1 tbsp nutella
1 tbsp strawberry jam
1 tbsp chopped nuts
13 wonton wrappers
1/2 tsp sugar
nonstick cooking spray

Directions
1. Set your oven to 350 degrees F before doing anything else and line a baking sheet with the parchment paper.
2. In a bowl, add the jam, nutella and banana and the jam and mix until smooth.
3. Place about 1 tsp of the mixture in the center of each wonton wrapper, followed by the nuts.
4. With wet fingers, moisten the edges of each wrapper and then, fold over the filling in a triangle shape.
5. Now, with your fingers, press the edges to seal completely.
6. In a deep skillet, add the oil over medium-high heat and cook until heated through.
7. In the bottom of the prepared baking sheet, arrange the wonton wrappers.
8. Spray each wrapper with the cooking spray and dust with the sugar.
9. Cook in the oven for about 30 minutes 11-15 minutes.
10. Enjoy hot with your favorite topping.

Wonton
Noodle Wok

Prep Time: 5 mins
Total Time: 15 mins

Servings per Recipe: 1
Calories	213.5
Fat	8.4g
Cholesterol	0.0mg
Sodium	53.2mg
Carbohydrates	22.3g
Protein	20.1g

Ingredients

3 oz. Asian noodles
1 large portobello mushroom, sliced
1 C. cabbage, shredded
1 C. bean sprouts
1/2 medium onion, sliced
1 stalk bok choy, chopped
6 oz. firm tofu, cubed
5 tbsp maggi seasoning
1 tbsp red pepper flakes

Directions

1. Cook the wonton noodles until al dente as suggested on the package.
2. Place a lightly greased skillet over medium-high heat until heated through.
3. Add the vegetables and sauté for about 4 minutes.
4. Add the tofu, seasoning and red pepper flakes and sauté for about 3 minutes.
5. Add the cooked wonton noodles and sauté for about 1-2 minutes.
6. Remove from the heat and keep aside for about 4-5 minutes.
7. Enjoy warm.

HOT MANGO
Wonton Bites

Prep Time: 20 mins
Total Time: 30 mins

Servings per Recipe: 48
Calories   20.5
Fat   0.9g
Cholesterol   9.8mg
Sodium   69.3mg
Carbohydrates   1.8g
Protein   1.1g

Ingredients
12 wonton wrappers, each cut into 4
squares
vegetable oil
1/2 C. mayonnaise
2 tbsp chopped fresh cilantro
5 tsp lime juice
2 tsp mango chutney, see appendix
1/4 tsp Thai green chili paste, see appendix
12 oz. peeled cooked medium shrimp,

chopped
cilantro leaves

Directions
1. In a bowl, add the mayonnaise, chutney, lime juice, chopped fresh cilantro and curry paste and beat until smooth.

2. Add the shrimp, salt and pepper and gently, stir to combine.

3. Cover the bowl and place in the fridge to chill.

4. Set your oven to 325 degrees F before doing anything else.

5. Arrange the wonton squares onto a smooth surface and coat 1 side of each with the oil.

6. Place 1 wonton square into 1 of each mini muffin cup, oiled side down and press to fit in a cup shape.

7. Cook in the oven for about 10 minutes.

8. Remove from the oven and keep onto a wire rack to cool completely.

9. Carefully, remove each cup from the muffin pan and place onto the wire rack to cool completely.

10. Place about 1 tsp of the shrimp salad into each wonton cup and enjoy with a garnishing of the cilantro leaves.

Wontons
Vegan with Dijon Duck Sauce

🥣 Prep Time: 20 mins
🕐 Total Time: 35 mins

Servings per Recipe: 1
Calories	101.3
Fat	6.3g
Cholesterol	0.0mg
Sodium	194.0mg
Carbohydrates	11.1g
Protein	1.3g

Ingredients

Sauce
1/2 C. apricot jam
1 tbsp Dijon mustard
Wontons
4 tbsp canola oil, divided
5 oz. shiitake mushrooms, stemmed and sliced
1/2 C. cashews
2 scallions, trimmed and sliced
1/4 C. shredded carrot
2 garlic cloves, minced

1/2 tsp grated ginger
2 tbsp soy sauce
wonton wrapper

Directions

1. For the sauce: in a pot, add all the ingredients over medium heat and cook until well combined, mixing frequently.
2. Transfer the sauce into a bowl and keep aside to cool.
3. For the filling: in a skillet, add 2 tbsp of the oil over medium-high heat and cook until heated through.
4. Add the mushrooms until and stir fry for about 6-7 minutes.
5. Add the cashews, carrot, scallion, ginger, garlic and soy sauce and cook for about 5 minutes.
6. Remove from the heat and keep aside to cool slightly.
7. In a blender, add the mushroom mixture and pulse until a slightly smooth mixture is formed.
8. Arrange the wonton wrappers onto a smooth surface.
9. Place about 2 tsp of the mixture in the center of each wonton wrapper.
10. With wet fingers, moisten the edges of each wrapper and then, fold over the filling in a triangle shape.
11. Now, with your fingers, press the edges to seal completely.
12. In a deep skillet, add 2 tbsp of the oil over medium-high heat and cook until heated through.
13. Add the wontons in batches and cook until golden brown.
14. Gradually, add 1/2-inch deep water and cook, covered for about 5 minutes.
15. Carefully, turn the wontons and cook until golden brown.

WONTONS
Georgia

Prep Time: 10 mins
Total Time: 15 mins

Servings per Recipe: 1
Calories	38.1
Fat	1.2g
Cholesterol	3.5mg
Sodium	98.5mg
Carbohydrates	5.0g
Protein	1.6g

Ingredients
15 wonton wrappers
6 tbsp diced peaches
2 oz. blue cheese, crumbled
1/2 tsp chopped sage leaf
cooking oil

Directions
1. Arrange the wonton wrappers onto a smooth surface.
2. Place the peach pieces in the center of each wonton wrapper, followed by the blue cheese and sage.
3. With wet fingers, moisten the edges of each wrapper and then, fold over the filling in a triangle shape.
4. Now, with your fingers, press the edges to seal completely.
5. In a deep skillet, add 3-inch of the oil and cook until its temperature reaches to 325 degrees F.
6. Add the wontons in batches and cook for about 2-3 minutes.
7. With a slotted spoon, transfer the wontons onto a paper towel-lined plate to drain.
8. Enjoy hot.

Southwest
Wonton Toppers

Prep Time: 10 mins
Total Time: 30 mins

Servings per Recipe: 8
Calories	164.9
Fat	5.8g
Cholesterol	43.8mg
Sodium	324.2mg
Carbohydrates	11.0g
Protein	16.2g

Ingredients
2 C. cooked boneless skinless chicken breasts, diced
1/2 C. enchilada sauce
2 scallions, sliced
1 tbsp diced canned green chili pepper, drained
16 wonton wrappers
1/4 lb. reduced-fat Monterey Jack pepper cheese, shredded

Directions
1. Set your oven to 375 degrees F before doing anything else and lightly, grease 8 cups of a muffin pan.
2. In a bowl, add the chicken, scallions, chilies and enchilada sauce and mix until well combined.
3. Place 1 wrapper into 1 of each prepared muffin cup and press to fit in a cup shape.
4. .
5. Divide half of the chicken mixture into each wonton cup evenly, followed by half of the cheese.
6. Place 1 wonton wrapper on top of each cup and press slightly.
7. Top with the remaining chicken mixture, followed by the remaining cheese.
8. Cook in the oven for about 18-20 minutes.
9. Remove from the oven and keep aside to cool for about 5 minutes.
10. Carefully, remove from the muffin pan and enjoy.

ALTERNATIVE
Wonton Soup

Prep Time: 2 hr
Total Time: 2 hr 30 mins

Servings per Recipe: 6

Calories	242.3
Fat	2.4g
Cholesterol	5.7mg
Sodium	373.9mg
Carbohydrates	47.4g
Protein	8.3g

Ingredients

Wontons
1 C. red bell pepper, diced
1 1/2 lb. eggplants, diced
1 tsp ginger, crushed
3 tbsp cilantro, minced
1/2 tbsp sesame seeds, toasted
1 tsp hot sesame oil
salt
pepper
48 wonton wrappers

Soup Base
1 C. water
6 C. vegetable broth
1 1/2 tbsp lemon juice
1/2 tbsp lemon zest
1/2 C. snow peas, julienned
1/2 C. spinach, chiffonade
1 tbsp cilantro, julienned
1 green pepper, sliced crossways

Directions

1. In a steamer, add the eggplant and bell pepper and steam for about 8 minutes.
2. Transfer the vegetables into a bowl and with a potato masher, mash them.
3. Add the cilantro, ginger, sesame oil, sesame seeds, salt and pepper and mix until well combined.
4. Place about 2 tsp of the mixture in the center of each wonton wrapper.
5. With wet fingers, moisten the edges of each wrapper and then, fold over the filling in a triangle shape.
6. Now, with your fingers, press the edges to seal completely.
7. In a pan, add the broth, water, lemon juice and lemon zest and cook until boiling.
8. Cook for about 3 minutes.
9. Stir in the spinach, snow peas, green pepper and cilantro and remove from the heat.
10. Meanwhile, in another pan of the boiling water, cook the wontons in batches for about 3 minutes.
11. Divide the wontons into serving bowls evenly.
12. Top with the hot broth and enjoy.

Yuan's
Veggie Wontons

🍲 Prep Time: 10 mins
🕐 Total Time: 15 mins

Servings per Recipe: 6
Calories	80.7
Fat	0.4g
Cholesterol	2.4m g
Sodium	153.6mg
Carbohydrates	16.1g
Protein	2.7g

Ingredients
1 C. chopped shiitake mushroom
1 C. chopped oyster mushroom
1 tbsp chopped Thai basil
2 green onions, sliced
2 tsp soy sauce
2 garlic cloves, crushed
20 wonton wrappers
2 tbsp water
soy sauce

Directions
1. In a bowl, add the mushrooms, onion, basil, garlic and soy sauce and mix well.
2. With a 3-inch cutter, cut rounds from each wonton wrapper.
3. Place about 2 tsp of mushroom mixture in the center of each wonton round.
4. With wet fingers, moisten the edges of each wrapper and then, fold over the filling in a semicircle.
5. Now, with your fingers, press the edges to seal completely.
6. Arrange the wontons into a baking paper lined bamboo steamer.
7. Arrange the steamer over a pan of simmering water.
8. Cover the pan and steam for about 4-5 minutes.
9. Enjoy hot alongside the soy sauce.

CHICAGO
Pizza Poppers

Prep Time: 20 min
Total Time: 30 mins

Servings per Recipe: 1
Calories   54.5
Fat   2.6g
Cholesterol   8.6mg
Sodium   122.5mg
Carbohydrates   4.9g
Protein   2.5g

Ingredients
24 wonton wrappers
2 oz. pepperoni, 24 slices
2 Roma tomatoes, seeded and chopped
1 scallion, sliced
salt
cracked black pepper
4 oz. Fontina cheese, grated
1 tsp dried thyme

Directions
1. Set your oven to 375 degrees F before doing anything else.
2. Place 1 wrapper into 1 of each ungreased muffin cup and press to fit in a cup shape.
3. Cook in the oven for about 6-7 minutes.
4. Remove from oven and keep onto the wire rack to cool.
5. Now, set your oven to 350 degrees F.
6. In a bowl, add the tomato pieces, scallion, a little salt and black pepper and toss to coat well.
7. Fold each pepperoni slice into fourths.
8. In the bottom of each baked wonton cup, place 1 folded pepperoni slice, followed by the tomato mixture, Fontina cheese and dried thyme.
9. Cook in the oven for about 2-3 minutes.
10. Enjoy warm.

Hawaiian
Wonton Cups

🥣 Prep Time: 10 mins
🕐 Total Time: 35 mins

Servings per Recipe: 12
Calories   189.6
Fat   8.4g
Cholesterol   11.6mg
Sodium   168.6mg
Carbohydrates   27.4g
Protein   2.7g

Ingredients
vegetable oil cooking spray
24 wonton wrappers
1 (15 oz.) cans mangoes, drained
1 (15 oz.) cans pineapple tidbits, drained
1/2 C. macadamia nuts, chopped and toasted
1/3 C. flour
1/4 C. crystallized ginger, chopped
1/4 C. sugar
1/4 tsp salt
1/4 C. butter

Directions
1. Set your oven to 375 degrees F before doing anything else and lightly, grease 12 cups of a muffin pan.
2. Place 1 wrapper into 1 of each prepared mini muffin cup and press to fit in a cup shape.
3. In a bowl, mix together the pineapple and mango pieces.
4. In another bowl, add the flour, nuts, sugar, ginger and salt and mix well.
5. With a pastry cutter, cut the butter until a coarse crumb like mixture is formed.
6. Place the mango mixture into each wonton cup about 3/4 full and top each with the crumb mixture.
7. Cook in the oven for about 25 minutes.
8. Enjoy warm.

WONTON TURKEY
Toppers with Wasabi Aioli

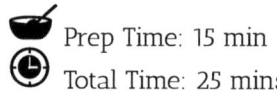

Prep Time: 15 min
Total Time: 25 mins

Servings per Recipe: 1

Calories	2022.2
Fat	44.3g
Cholesterol	399.4mg
Sodium	4082.2mg
Carbohydrates	267.3g
Protein	125.7g

Ingredients
1 (16 oz.) packages wonton wrappers
1 lb. ground turkey
2 stalks green onions, minced
2 fresh garlic cloves, minced
fresh ginger, minced
6 tsp low sodium soy sauce
pepper
Wasabi Aioli
mayonnaise
wasabi powder

Directions
1. For the wasabi aioli: in a bowl, add the mayonnaise and wasabi powder and mix well.
2. Refrigerate before using.
3. Set your oven to 350 degrees F and lightly, grease cups of a mini muffin pan.
4. Place 1 wrapper into 1 of each prepared mini muffin cup and press to fit in a cup shape.
5. Cook in the oven for about 10-12 minutes.
6. In a bowl, add the turkey, ginger, garlic, onion, soy sauce and pepper and mix well.
7. Heat a skillet over medium heat and cook the turkey mixture until cooked through.
8. Place desired amount of the turkey mixture into each cooked wonton cup and enjoy with a topping of the wasabi mayo.

55 Dragon Wontons

Prep Time: 15 mins
Total Time: 30 mins

Servings per Recipe: 6
Calories	247.3
Fat	7.9g
Cholesterol	3.6mg
Sodium	337.0mg
Carbohydrates	31.6g
Protein	13.6g

Ingredients
1 3/4 C. shelled frozen edamame
1 tbsp minced ginger
1 tsp lemon juice
1/4-1/2 tsp salt
1 tbsp minced chives
1 tbsp vegetable oil
30 wonton wrappers
cilantro leaf
soy sauce

Directions
1. Prepare the edamame as suggested on the package.
2. Drain the edamame, reserving 1/2 C. of the cooking liquid in a bowl.
3. In another bowl, reserve 3/4 C. of the edamame.
4. In a food processor, add the remaining edamame, ginger, salt, lemon juice and 1/3-1/2 C. of the reserved cooking liquid and pulse until smooth.
5. Place the pureed edamame mixture into a bowl with the reserved edamame and chives and mix well.
6. Place about 1 tsp of the mixture in the center of each wonton wrapper, followed by 1 cilantro leaf.
7. With wet fingers, moisten the edges of each wrapper and then, fold over the filling in a triangle shape.
8. Now, with your fingers, press the edges to seal completely.
9. In a pan, add water, oil and some salt and cook until boiling.
10. Add the wontons in batches and cook for about 2 minutes.
11. enjoy alongside the soy sauce.

SWEET WONTONS
New Zealand

Prep Time: 20 min
Total Time: 30 mins

Servings per Recipe: 8
Calories	161.3
Fat	6.6g
Cholesterol	9.0mg
Sodium	96.9mg
Carbohydrates	23.4g
Protein	2.4g

Ingredients
2 tbsp sugar
2 tsp cinnamon
16 wonton wrappers
5 tbsp nutella
1 banana, ripe, sliced
2 tbsp unsalted butter

Directions
1. Set your oven to 350 degrees F before doing anything else and line a baking sheet with the parchment paper.
2. In a bowl, add the cinnamon and sugar and mix well.
3. Arrange the wonton wrappers onto a smooth surface.
4. Place 1 tsp of the Nutella in the center of each wrapper, followed by 2 banana slices.
5. With wet fingers, moisten the edges of each wrapper and then, fold over the filling in a triangle shape.
6. Now, with your fingers, press the edges to seal completely.
7. In the bottom of the prepared baking sheet, arrange the wontons.
8. Coat each wonton with the melted butter and dust with the cinnamon sugar.
9. Cook in the oven for about 8-10 minutes.
10. Enjoy warm.

Wonton Crispers with Chinese Ceviche

🥣 Prep Time: 10 mins
🕐 Total Time: 16 mins

Servings per Recipe: 24
Calories	19.8
Fat	0.5g
Cholesterol	0.3mg
Sodium	149.1mg
Carbohydrates	3.0g
Protein	0.7g

Ingredients

1 C. diced cucumber
1/2 C. chopped red bell pepper
1/2 C. green onion
1/3 C. chopped cilantro
2 tbsp light soy sauce
1 tbsp rice vinegar
1 garlic clove
1/2 tsp dark sesame oil
1/4 tsp dried red pepper flakes
1 tbsp light soy sauce

2 tsp canola oil
1/2 tsp sugar
1/4 tsp garlic salt
12 wonton wrappers, halved diagonally

Directions

1. For the salsa: in a bowl, add the cucumber, bell pepper, green onion, garlic, cilantro, 2 tbsp of the soy sauce, vinegar, sesame oil and red pepper flakes and mix well.
2. Place I the fridge to chill completely.
3. Set your oven to 375 degrees F and grease a baking sheet.
4. In a bowl, add the canola oil, 1 tbsp of the soy sauce, sugar and garlic salt and mix well.
5. In the bottom of the prepared baking sheet, arrange the wonton wrappers and coat both sides of each with the soy sauce mixture.
6. Cook in the oven for about 4-6 minutes.
7. Enjoy alongside the salsa.

SORBET
Wontons Summers

Prep Time: 20 min
Total Time: 40 mins

Servings per Recipe: 8
Calories	735.2
Fat	58.6g
Cholesterol	1.4mg
Sodium	130.2mg
Carbohydrates	52.4g
Protein	3.7g

Ingredients
2 C. canola oil
16 wonton wrappers
1/2 C. sugar
1 tbsp ground ginger
3 pints sorbet, your choice of flavors
1 pint raspberry
1/2 C. roasted pistachios, chopped

Directions
1. In a bowl, add the ginger and sugar and mix.
2. In a Dutch oven, add the oil and cook until heated through.
3. Add the wontons in batches and cook for about 1-2 minutes, flipping once half way through.
4. With a slotted spoon, transfer the wontons onto a paper towel-lined plate to drain.
5. Keep aside to cool.
6. Coat each wonton with the sugar mixture.
7. With an ice cream scooper, create balls from the sorbet.
8. Arrange the sorbet balls onto a rimmed baking sheet and freeze until firm.
9. Arrange 2 fried wontons onto each serving plate and top each with the sorbet, berries and nuts.
10. Enjoy.

Italian
Wontons

🍲 Prep Time: 40 m..
🕐 Total Time: 40 min.

Servings per Recipe: 20
Calories   21.3
Fat   1.2g
Cholesterol   3.1mg
Sodium   64.0mg
Carbohydrates   1.7g
Protein   0.9g

Ingredients
2 2/3 C. frozen peas
1/3 C. grated parmigiano-reggiano cheese
2 tsp chopped mint
1/2 tsp salt
1/2 tsp pepper
about 64 wonton wrappers
1/4 C. unsalted butter, melted

Directions
1. In a pan, add the water and some salt and cook until boiling.
2. Add the peas and cook for about 4 minutes.
3. Drain the peas well and keep aside to cool slightly.
4. In a blender, add the cooked peas and pulse until pureed.
5. Transfer the pureed peas into a bowl with the mint, cheese, salt and pepper and mix well.
6. Place a rounded tsp of the filling in center of each of 32 wrappers.
7. With wet fingers, moisten the edges of each wrapper.
8. Cover each with 1 of the remaining wrappers.
9. Now, with your fingers, press the edges to seal completely.
10. In a pan, add the water and some salt and cook until boiling.
11. Add the wontons in batches and cook for about 2-3 minutes.
12. With a slotted spoon, transfer the wontons onto a platter and drizzle with the butter.
13. Enjoy with a topping of the cheese and pepper.

ALTERNATIVE
Homemade Gyoza

Prep Time: 30 min
Total Time: 30 mins

Servings per Recipe: 4
Calories	227.5
Fat	0.6g
Cholesterol	0.0mg
Sodium	292.5mg
Carbohydrates	47.6g
Protein	6.4g

Ingredients
2 C. all-purpose flour
1/2 tsp salt
1/2 C. warm water
cornstarch

Directions
1. In a bowl, add the flour and salt and mix well.
2. Slowly, add the warm water and mix until a stiff dough forms.
3. Place the dough onto a lightly floured surface and with your hands, knead until a smooth and elastic dough is formed.
4. With a kitchen towel, cover the dough for about 20 minutes.
5. Cut the dough into 4 equal sized portions.
6. With a floured rolling pin, roll each dough portion into a 12-inch square.
7. With a sharp knife, cut 3-inch squares from each dough portion.
8. Sprinkle the dough squared with a little cornstarch.
9. Enjoy these wontons with your favorite filling.

Monterey Moroccan Open-Faced Wontons

Prep Time: 25 mins
Total Time: 35 mins

Servings per Recipe: 12
Calories	125.7
Fat	3.6g
Cholesterol	5.9mg
Sodium	224.7mg
Carbohydrates	18.4g
Protein	5.0g

Ingredients

24 wonton wrappers
Filling
1 (15 oz.) cans garbanzo beans, rinsed well
3 tbsp sesame seeds
2 tbsp onions, chopped
1-2 garlic clove
2 tbsp lemon juice
2 tbsp water
1 tsp olive oil
Garnish

2 oz. shredded Monterey Jack cheese
2 tbsp red bell peppers, chopped

Directions

1. Set your oven to 350 degrees F before doing anything else and lightly, grease 24 cups of a mini muffin pan.
2. Place 1 wrapper into 1 of each prepared muffin cup and press to fit in a cup shape.
3. Spray each wrapper cup with the cooking spray lightly.
4. Cook in the oven for about 5-8 minutes.
5. Remove from the oven and keep aside to cool slightly.
6. Carefully, remove the wonton cups from muffin pan.
7. Meanwhile, for the filling: in a blender, add all the ingredients and pulse until smooth.
8. Place the pureed mixture into a pan and cook until heated through.
9. Remove from the heat.
10. Place about 1 tbsp of the filling into each wonton cup, followed by the cheese and bell pepper.
11. Cook in the oven for about 3-4 minutes.
12. Enjoy hot.

PAN FRIED
Wontons

Prep Time: 30 min
Total Time: 60 mins

Servings per Recipe: 6
Calories	372.0
Fat	17.5g
Cholesterol	112.7mg
Sodium	868.6mg
Carbohydrates	36.4g
Protein	16.4g

Ingredients
20 square wonton wrappers
Filling
12 oz. shrimp, veins removed
1 tbsp sesame oil
1 tbsp sugar
1 tbsp parsley, chopped
2 tsp garlic, chopped
2 tsp ginger root, chopped
3 tbsp carrots, minced, blanched
3 tbsp celery, minced, blanched

1-2 tsp salt
1/2 tsp black pepper
3/4 C. brown rice, cooked
Flavored Oil
2 bunches scallions, green only
2 tsp rice vinegar
2 tbsp peanut oil
4 tbsp vegetable oil
1/2 tsp salt

Directions
1. For the scallion oil: in a pan of the boiling water, add the scallions and cook slightly.
2. Drain the scallions well.
3. In a food processor, add the vinegar, scallions and salt and pulse until smooth.
4. While the motor is running, slowly add the oil and pulse until well combined.
5. In a food processor, add the shrimp, parsley, ginger, garlic, oil, sugar, salt and pepper and pulse until a slightly chunky mixture is formed.
6. Transfer the shrimp mixture into a bowl with the cooked rice and vegetables and mix well.
7. Place about desired amount of the mixture in the center of each wonton wrapper.
8. With wet fingers, moisten the edges of each wrapper and then, fold over the filling in a triangle shape.
9. Now, with your fingers, press the edges to seal completely.
10. In a deep skillet, add a little oil and cook until heated through.
11. Add the wontons and cook until golden brown.
12. carefully, flip the wontons.
13. Add enough water to cover the bottom of the skillet and steam, covered for about 4-5 minutes.
14. Transfer the wontons onto a platter and enjoy with a drizzling of the scallion oil.

Fresh Herbed
Wontons

🍲 Prep Time: 30 mins
🕐 Total Time: 40 mins

Servings per Recipe: 4
Calories   97.8
Fat   0.7g
Cholesterol   18.9mg
Sodium   140.6mg
Carbohydrates   13.0g
Protein   9.2g

Ingredients

2 coriander roots, washed, chopped
20 coriander leaves, washed, dried
2 garlic cloves, chopped
1 pinch flaked sea salt
1 large skinless chicken breast, chopped
2 green onions, sliced
2 tbsp soy sauce
10 - 20 wonton wrappers
100 ml cold water
vegetable oil

kitchen paper towels

Directions

1. With the mortar and pestle, mash the coriander roots, garlic and a little salt into a paste.
2. In a bowl, add the chicken, spring onions, coriander leaves, garlic paste and soy sauce and mix well.
3. Place about 1 tsp of the mixture in the center of each wonton wrapper.
4. With wet fingers, moisten the edges of each wrapper and then, fold over the filling in a triangle shape.
5. Now, with your fingers, press the edges to seal completely.
6. In a deep skillet, add the oil and cook until heated through.
7. Add the wontons in batches and cook for about 2 minutes.
8. With a slotted spoon, transfer the wontons onto a paper towel-lined plate to drain.
9. Enjoy alongside your favorite sauce.

CALIFORNIA
Wontons

Prep Time: 15 min
Total Time: 35 mins

Servings per Recipe: 1
Calories   57.8
Fat   3.1g
Cholesterol   5.1mg
Sodium   48.8mg
Carbohydrates   6.5g
Protein   1.3g

Ingredients
4 large avocados
1 tbsp garlic powder
1/4 tsp dry dried chipotle powder
1 lime, juice
1 tbsp cilantro, chopped, no stems
kosher salt and black pepper
1 egg
48 wonton wrappers
peanut oil

Directions
1. In a bowl, add the avocados, garlic, cilantro, lime juice, salt, chipotle and pepper and toss to coat well.
2. Place desired amount of the mixture in the center of each wonton wrapper.
3. Coat the edges of each wrapper with the beaten egg and then, fold over the filling in a triangle shape.
4. Now, with your fingers, press the edges to seal completely.
5. In a deep skillet, add the oil and cook until its temperature reaches to 350 degrees F.
6. Add the wontons in batches and cook until golden brown from both sides.
7. With a slotted spoon, transfer the wontons onto a paper towel-lined plate to drain.
8. Enjoy warm.

Crab
Wontons

🥣 Prep Time: 45 mins
🕐 Total Time: 1 hr

Servings per Recipe: 8
Calories	94.7
Fat	6.9g
Cholesterol	18.1mg
Sodium	287.7mg
Carbohydrates	2.6g
Protein	5.5g

Ingredients

2 cans crab meat, drained and picked through
1 can baby shrimp, drained
1 (8 oz.) bags shredded cheese
2 tsp Worcestershire sauce
2 tsp Old Bay Seasoning
mayonnaise
1 package wonton
vegetable oil

Directions

1. In a bowl, add all the ingredients except the wrappers and oil and mix until well combined.
2. Arrange the wonton wrappers onto a smooth surface.
3. Place about 1 tsp of the mixture in the center of each wonton wrapper.
4. With wet fingers, moisten the edges of each wrapper and then, fold over the filling in a triangle shape.
5. Now, with your fingers, press the edges to seal completely.
6. In a deep skillet, add the oil and cook until its temperature reaches to 350 degrees F.
7. Add the wontons in batches and cook until golden brown from both sides.
8. With a slotted spoon, transfer the wontons onto a paper towel-lined plate to drain.
9. Enjoy warm.

OPEN
Wonton Salad

🥣 Prep Time: 12 min
🕐 Total Time: 20 mins

Servings per Recipe: 4
Calories	161.9
Fat	8.9g
Cholesterol	1.4mg
Sodium	148.6mg
Carbohydrates	17.0g
Protein	5.2g

Ingredients
8 wonton wrappers
deep frying oil
2 gem lettuce, cut into 1 inch size
1/2 cucumber, halved, seeded and diced
2 tomatoes, peeled, seeded and diced
1 hard-cooked egg white, diced
Dressing
1 tbsp crunchy peanut butter
1/2 C. coconut milk
1 tbsp sugar

3 drops lemon juice
3 drops Tabasco sauce
salt & ground pepper

Directions
1. For the peanut dressing: in a pot, add the coconut milk, peanut butter and sugar over low heat and cook until just combined, stirring continuously.
2. Remove from the heat and stir in the Tabasco sauce, lemon juice, salt and pepper.
3. Keep aside to cool.
4. Carefully, separate the wonton wrappers and then, cut each into 4 pieces.
5. In a deep skillet, add the oil and cook until heated through.
6. With a slotted spoon, transfer the wontons onto a paper towel-lined plate to drain.
7. Divide the lettuce leaves onto plates and top with half of the peanut dressing, followed by the cucumber, tomatoes, eggs and wonton crisps.
8. Enjoy with a drizzling of the remaining dressing.

Hot Mushroom
Wontons with Topical Dumpling Sauce

Prep Time: 30 mins
Total Time: 47 mins

Servings per Recipe: 10
Calories   155.7
Fat   8.6g
Cholesterol   2.1mg
Sodium   375.1mg
Carbohydrates   16.3g
Protein   3.1g

Ingredients

Sauce
1/2 C. dried mango
1 tbsp tamari
2 tbsp mirin
1 tbsp rice vinegar
1 tsp grated gingerroot
1/4 tsp chili paste, see appendix
Wontons
1 C. grated carrot
1/2 C. sliced mushroom

1 C. shredded Napa cabbage
6 tbsp toasted sesame oil
1/4 C. chopped scallion
1/2 tbsp grated ginger
1/2 tbsp curry powder
1 tbsp mirin
1 tbsp tamari
30 small square uncooked wonton wrappers

Directions

1. Set your oven to 375 degrees F before doing anything else and lightly, grease a baking sheet.
2. For the dipping sauce: in a bowl, add the mango and 1 C. of the boiling water and keep aside for about 30 minutes.
3. Through a strainer, strain the mangoes, reserving 1/2 C. of the soaking water.
4. In the bowl of the soaking water, add the ginger, mirin, vinegar, tamari and chili paste and mix well.
5. For the filling: in pot, add 2 tbsp of the oil over medium heat and cook until heated through.
6. Add the mushroom, cabbage and carrots and stir fry for about 5 minutes.
7. Stir in the scallion, ginger, mirin, tamari and curry powder and remove from the heat.
8. Arrange the wonton wrappers onto a smooth surface and coat with a thin layer of the sesame oil.
9. Place about 1 tbsp of the filling mixture in the center of each wonton wrapper.
10. With wet fingers, moisten the edges of each wrapper and then, fold over the filling in a triangle shape.
11. Now, with your fingers, press the edges to seal completely and coat the top of each with the oil.
12. In the bottom of the prepared baking sheet, arrange the wontons.
13. Cook in the oven for about 12 minutes, flipping once half way through.
14. Enjoy the wontons alongside the dipping sauce.

SEAFOOD
Wonton Platter

 Prep Time: 10 min
Total Time: 35 mins

Servings per Recipe: 12
Calories   122.8
Fat   6.8g
Cholesterol   37.3mg
Sodium   415.1mg
Carbohydrates   10.8g
Protein   4.4g

Ingredients
24 Chinese wonton wrappers
vegetable oil
1 (8 oz.) packages softened cream cheese
1 tbsp minced garlic
1 tsp salt
24 prawns, cooked, tails removed
1/2 C. chopped green onion, plus
1/4 C. green onion

Directions
1. Set your oven to 350 degrees F before doing anything else.
2. Place 1 wrapper into 1 of each ungreased muffin cup and press to fit in a cup shape.
3. Cook in the oven for about 10 minutes.
4. remove the muffin tin from the oven and keep aside to cool slightly.
5. In a bowl, add the cream cheese, 1/2 C. of the green onions, garlic and salt and beat until smooth.
6. Place about 1 tbsp of the cream cheese mixture in each wonton cup.
7. Cook in the oven for about 15 minutes.
8. Remove from the oven and immediately top each cup with 1 prawn.
9. Enjoy warm with a garnishing of the remaining green onion.

Fried
Wonton Wafers

🥣 Prep Time: 30 mins
🕐 Total Time: 45 mins

Servings per Recipe: 1
Calories	169.9
Fat	4.7g
Cholesterol	0.7mg
Sodium	83.2mg
Carbohydrates	31.5g
Protein	2.6g

Ingredients
1 1/2 C. chopped prunes,
1 C. chopped dried apricot
1 1/2 C. packed brown sugar
1 1/2 C. flaked coconut
1 C. chopped almonds
24 wonton skins
vegetable oil

Directions
1. For the filling: in a bowl, add the apricots, prunes, almonds, coconut and brown sugar and mix well.
2. Place about 2 tsp of the mixture in the center of each wonton wrapper.
3. With wet fingers, moisten the edges of each wrapper and then, fold over the filling in a triangle shape.
4. Now, with your fingers, press the edges to seal completely.
5. In a deep skillet, add 1-1-1/2-inch of the oil and cook until its temperature reaches to 360 degrees F.
6. Add the wontons in batches and cook for about 2 minutes, flipping once half way through.
7. With a slotted spoon, transfer the wontons onto a paper towel-lined plate to drain.
8. Enjoy warm.

MONTEREY
Wonton Cups

Prep Time: 10 min
Total Time: 15 mins

Servings per Recipe: 24
Calories   54.5
Fat   2.3g
Cholesterol   5.0mg
Sodium   100.4mg
Carbohydrates   6.2g
Protein   2.3g

Ingredients
1 (9 oz.) boxes green giant frozen spinach
24 wonton skins
1 (7 oz.) cans old el paso chopped green
chilies
1/3 C. reduced-fat mayonnaise
3/4 C. shredded Monterey Jack and cheddar
cheese blend

Directions
1. Set your oven to 350 degrees F before doing anything else.
2. Prepare the spinach as suggested on the package.
3. Drain the spinach well and keep aside to cool.
4. Then, squeeze the moisture from the spinach.
5. Place 1 wrapper into 1 of each 24 ungreased standard sized muffin cup and press to fit in a cup shape.
6. Cook in the oven for about 7-10 minutes.
7. Meanwhile, in a bowl, add the spinach, green chilies, 1/4 C. of the cheese and mayonnaise and mix until well combined.
8. Place about 1 tbsp of the spinach mixture into each wonton cup and top with the cheese evenly.
9. Cook in the oven for about 5-7 minutes.
10. Enjoy warm.

Chicken Wontons with Thai Sauce

🥣 Prep Time: 30 mins
🕐 Total Time: 30 mins

Servings per Recipe: 1
Calories   150
Fat   39.6
Cholesterol   1.2g
Sodium   0.7mg
Carbohydrates   99.3mg
Protein   5.8g

Ingredients

1 C. chicken meat, cooked and diced
4 green onions, diced
1 C. cabbage, shredded
2 tbsp cilantro, chopped
2 tsp brown sugar
1 tbsp hoisin sauce
1 tsp sesame oil
36 wonton wrappers
peanut oil
1/2 C. chicken broth

2 tbsp hoisin sauce
2 tbsp sesame oil
2 tsp soy sauce
1 tbsp creamy peanut butter
1 tsp cornstarch

Directions

1. In a bowl, add the chicken meat, cabbage, onions, cilantro, brown sugar, hoisin sauce and sesame oil and mix until well combined.
2. Place about 1 tsp of the mixture in the center of each wonton wrapper.
3. With wet fingers, moisten the edges of each wrapper and then, fold over the filling in a triangle shape.
4. Now, with your fingers, press the edges to seal completely.
5. In a deep skillet, add the oil and cook until its temperature reaches to 375 degrees F.
6. Add the wontons in batches and cook until golden brown from both sides.
7. With a slotted spoon, transfer the wontons onto a paper towel-lined plate to drain.
8. Meanwhile, for the sauce: in a bowl, add the chicken broth, hoisin sauce, sesame oil, soy sauce, peanut butter and cornstarch and cook until boiling.
9. Cook for about 1 minute, beating continuously.
10. Enjoy the wontons alongside the sauce.

SAVORY LITTLE
Wonton Pie

Prep Time: 10 min
Total Time: 1 hr 5 mins

Servings per Recipe: 1
Calories   653.7
Fat   28.0g
Cholesterol   370.3mg
Sodium   1244.2mg
Carbohydrates   67.9g
Protein   32.7g

Ingredients
24 wonton wrappers
1 C. broccoli, chopped
3/4 C. mushrooms, diced
1/2 C. sweet red pepper, diced
1/4 C. onion, chopped
2 tsp vegetable oil
3 eggs
1 tbsp water
2 tsp dried parsley flakes
1/4 tsp salt

1/4 tsp dried thyme
1/4 tsp white pepper
1 dash cayenne pepper
3/4 C. cheddar cheese, shredded

Directions
1. Set your oven to 350 degrees F before doing anything else and grease cups of a muffin pan.
2. Place 1 wrapper into 1 of each prepared mini muffin cup and press to fit in a cup shape.
3. Spray each cup with the nonstick cooking spray lightly.
4. Cook in the oven for about for 5 minutes.
5. Remove the wontons from the oven and keep aside to cool slightly.
6. Carefully, remove from the muffin cups and arrange onto baking sheets.
7. Spray each cup with the cooking spray lightly.
8. Cook in the oven for about for 5 minutes.
9. Meanwhile, in a nonstick skillet, add the oil over medium heat and cook until heated through.
10. Add the onion, mushrooms, broccoli and sweet pepper and onion and stir fry for about 4-5 minutes.
11. In a bowl, add the water, eggs, parsley, thyme, salt, cayenne and white pepper and beat until well combined.
12. Add the egg mixture into the skillet and cook for about 4-5 minutes.
13. Remove from the heat and stir in the cheddar cheese until well combined.
14. Place about 1 tbsp of the mixture into each wonton cup.
15. Cook in the oven for about for 5 minutes.
16. Enjoy warm.

New England
Shrimp Wontons

🍲 Prep Time: 30 mins
🕐 Total Time: 40 mins

Servings per Recipe: 16
Calories	143.2
Fat	1.8g
Cholesterol	48.4mg
Sodium	441.5mg
Carbohydrates	20.8g
Protein	10.3g

Ingredients

Wontons
1 lb. medium raw shrimp
4 garlic cloves
1 tsp ginger, minced
1 lime, juice and zest
1 C. plain fat-free yogurt
3 tbsp cream cheese
1 C. cooked white rice
2 tbsp scallions, chopped
2 tbsp cilantro, chopped
1/4 tsp crushed red pepper flakes

1 (12 oz.) packages wonton wrappers
peanut oil
Sauce
1/2 C. plain fat-free yogurt
1/4 C. soy sauce
1/4 C. lime juice
2 tbsp water
2 garlic cloves, mashed to paste with 1/2 tsp of salt
2 tsp cilantro, chopped
2 tbsp sugar
1/4 tsp hot red pepper flakes

Directions

1. In a blender, add the ginger, garlic, lime zest and juice and zest and pulse until well combined.
2. Transfer the ginger mixture into a bowl with the shrimp, cream cheese and yogurt and mix well.
3. In another bowl, add the rice, cilantro, scallion and red pepper flakes and mix well.
4. Add the shrimp mixture and gently, stir to combine.
5. Arrange the wonton wrappers onto a smooth surface.
6. Place about 1 tsp of the mixture in the center of wonton wrapper.
7. Place about 1 tbsp of the mixture in the center of each wonton wrapper.
8. With wet fingers, moisten the edges of each wrapper and then, fold over the filling in a triangle shape.
9. Now, with your fingers, press the edges to seal completely.
10. In a deep skillet, add the oil and cook until its temperature reaches to 375 degrees F.
11. Add the wontons in batches and cook until golden brown from both sides.
12. With a slotted spoon, transfer the wontons onto a paper towel-lined plate to drain.
13. Meanwhile, for dipping sauce: in a bowl, add all the ingredients and mix well.
14. Enjoy the wontons alongside the sauce.

SIMPLE HOMEMADE
Red Curry (Chili) Paste (Thailand Style)

Prep Time: 10 min
Total Time: 10 mins

Servings per Recipe: 1
Calories   300.4
Fat   3.5 g
Cholesterol   0 mg
Sodium   2368.8 mg
Carbohydrates   71.1 g
Protein   7.5 g

Ingredients
1/4 C. chopped scallion
1/4 C. chopped fresh cilantro
2 tbsps minced garlic
2 tbsps grated fresh gingerroot
1 tbsp freshly grated lemon rinds
1 tbsp brown sugar
1-2 fresh red chilies or 1-2 green chili, minced
3 tbsps fresh lemon juice
1 tbsp ground coriander

1 tsp turmeric
1/2 tsp salt

Directions
1. Add the following your food processor: scallion, cilantro, garlic, ginger root, lemons / lime, brown sugar, chilies, lemon / lime juice, coriander, turmeric, and salt.
2. Process and pulse everything until it becomes a smooth paste.
3. Enjoy.

Mango
Chutney

Prep Time: 20 mins
Total Time: 1 hr 5 mins

Servings per Recipe: 1
Calories   627.2
Fat   2.1g
Cholesterol   0.0mg
Sodium   3748.7mg
Carbohydrates   153.4g
Protein   4.2g

Ingredients
1 kg very firm mango
2 C. sugar
625 ml vinegar
1 (5 cm) pieces ginger, peeled
4 cloves garlic, peeled
2-4 tsps chili powder
4 tsps mustard seeds
8 tsps salt
1 C. raisins or 1 C. sultana

Directions
1. Peel the mango and then remove the pit and chop it.
2. In a pan, add sugar and vinegar, leaving about 20ml and simmer, stirring occasionally for about 10 minutes.
3. Meanwhile in a food processor, add remaining vinegar, garlic and ginger and pulse till a paste forms.
4. Transfer the paste into a pan and simmer, stirring continuously for about 10 minutes.
5. Stir in the mango and remaining ingredients and simmer, stirring occasionally for about 25 minutes or till desired thickness of chutney.
6. Transfer the chutney into hot sterilized jars and seal tightly and keep aside to cool.
7. This chutney can be stored in dark place for about 1 year but remember to refrigerate after opening.

ENJOY THE RECIPES?

KEEP ON COOKING
WITH 6 MORE FREE COOKBOOKS!

Visit our website and simply enter your email address to join the club and receive your 6 cookbooks.

http://booksumo.com/magnet

Printed in Great Britain
by Amazon